"Everyone, yes I said everyone, can change the world with a napkin and a Sharpie, and in his book Dan Roam shows you exactly how!"

—CARL RICHARDS,
author of *The Behavior Gap*
and *The One-Page Financial Plan*

DRAW TO WIN

DRAW
TO
WIN

A Crash Course on How to Lead, Sell, and Innovate with Your Visual Mind

DAN ROAM

Portfolio / Penguin

An imprint of Penguin Random House LLC
375 Hudson Street
New York, New York 10014

ISBN 9780399562990
Ebook ISBN 9780399563003
International edition ISBN: 9780735213418

Printed in the United States of America
4th Printing

Set in Mercury Text G1 with Verlag
Book design by Daniel Lagin

For my dad.
Thank you for the wings.

CONTENTS

DRAW TO WIN

THE KICKOFF

From the dawning of the day, the air is filled with countless images
for which the eye acts as magnet.

—LEONARDO DA VINCI

There's always room out there for the hand-drawn image.

—MATT GROENING

On June 29, 2007, after a year of writing, I finished *The Back of the Napkin*. I remember the date because I had to stop halfway through the last page so I could watch Steve Jobs launch the iPhone. It was a big day.

In the years since, I have been blessed with the opportunity to share my visual-thinking approach with hundreds of organizations, from Fortune 500 companies to inner-city schools. As I scan my computer, I see 723 different presentations I've delivered, containing 9,246 hand-drawn images. That's a lot of pictures.

Along the way, I've learned a few things:

■ Pictures help people learn, and the best pictures are the simplest.

- Simple can be hard, but having a process makes hard things easier.
- Hand-drawn pictures make people smile, and smiling people think better.
- Everyone can draw, even people who *know* they can't.

In this book, I will share with you the top ten lessons I've learned. The first two explain *why* you should draw. The next three show you *how* to draw. And the last five show you *what* to draw when you need to lead, sell, innovate, train, or just figure things out on your road to success.

If you've read my previous books, you'll see one or two familiar tools here, now refined through years of testing, along with a bunch of new tools. If you're new to my approach, welcome! You're about to see a whole new way of thinking.

Dan Roam
San Francisco, 2016

CHAPTER 1

DRAW LIKE YOUR LIFE DEPENDS ON IT

Let whoever may have attained to so much as to have the power of drawing know that he holds a great treasure.

—MICHELANGELO

Three Data Points That Point to Pictures

90% of the data in the world today has been created in the last two years alone.

—IBM, "WHAT IS BIG DATA?"

While researching a project recently, I was struck by three surprising data points. The first was from IBM, saying that 90 percent of all data collected in history has been generated in the last two years. The second was from Cisco, saying that 90 percent of all data transmitted online today is visual. The third came from my own work in corporate training, where I see that 90 percent of businesspeople have no idea how to effectively use visuals in their business.

90%-90%-90%. We're generating more data than ever, that data is overwhelmingly visual, and most of us don't know how to use images. No matter what business you're in, the future of your business is visual. To keep your business growing, you're going to have to get better at using pictures.

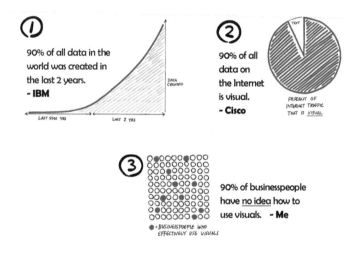

One More Data Point . . .

Then I came across one more data point, this time in *Entertainment Weekly*: Seven out of the top twenty bestselling books on Amazon in recent months were coloring books for adults. According to the *Boston Globe*, this "sudden, unexpected, and generally curious development" has become "*the* thing, as far as millions of rapt Americans are concerned."

I don't think it's sudden, unexpected, or curious at all. We've always been visual. Most businesspeople just forget that.

Drawing Is Our Oldest Technology

Thirty-two thousand years ago, your many-times-great-grandparents Oog and Aag drew pictures on the wall of a cave. They drew bison, a herd of horses, and many beautiful bulls. These drawings predate weapons, pots, jewelry, and most clothes.

OOG AND AAG AND THE
WORLD'S OLDEST TECHNOLOGIES

Your ancient ancestors had things to tell each other, and the technology they used to record it was drawing. That desire to share was so compelling that Oog and Aag's children and grandchildren and great-grandchildren kept going back to that *same* cave and drew the *same* pictures—for the next eight hundred years.

Adult drawing is "curious"? I don't think so. The only thing curious is why people in business don't draw more.

The Visual Is Back—and Here to Stay

Everyone online relies on pictures: Facebook, YouTube, Pinterest, Instagram, Snapchat, Tumblr; the greatest focus of social media is the *image*. This explosion of pictures isn't a millennials-powered fad disconnected from the world of business. It's the logical extension of those lines first drawn by Oog and Aag. Today we just have better technology.

Don't think of sharing images as the dumbing-down of society or as threatening to business; on the contrary, creating and sharing pictures is the most natural thing in the world.

The problem is that there are too many images that aren't very good, or good for you. Most pictures online are "lazy images." Cute cats, train wrecks, and sexy bodies have their appeal, but they appeal to your lowest-common-denominator brain; they distract and occupy your brain without leaving much value behind.

Good images—meaningful pictures that trigger deep thoughts, clarify complexity, and inspire insight—exist too but are fewer in number. That's not the fault of the pictures. The reason lazy images are so distracting is because the people who make them know that your brain loves to look at stuff. That's good to know—and we're going to take advantage of that too, but we're going to use that insight to turn your good ideas into better pictures.

Why is that important? Because, as Cisco reminds us, 90 percent of the data you see is visual.

The Conversation Is Now Visual

Always enter the conversation already taking place in the customer's mind.

—ROBERT COLLIER

If you walk through the office talking loudly to yourself, nobody will listen. But if you can enter the conversation that is already going on in your colleague's head, he or she will pay complete attention and invite you in. That's always been true.

What's different today is that now the conversation is visual. People's stories are visual. Shopping is visual. The news is visual. If you want to enter just about any conversation today, you need to be visual too. Learn to join the visual conversation and you will be seen and heard.

Don't Be Afraid of Drawing

Don't be the businessperson who says, "I can't draw; therefore, I'm not visual." That's a deceptive trap. It's deceptive because it assumes that drawing is difficult and that being visual is dependent on drawing. Neither is true. And it's a trap because it stops you from accessing the most powerful problem-solving part of your brain before you even know it exists. And that's not just silly; it's a huge roadblock.

What Is Drawing, Really?

I prefer drawing to talking. Drawing is faster, and leaves less room for lies.

—LE CORBUSIER

Just as writing is the recording mechanism of verbal thinking, drawing is the recording mechanism of visual thinking. Drawing is neither a mystery nor a secret talent; it's an attitude that says, "I am a visual creature and I am going to take advantage of that. I will draw to help me understand the world and I will keep drawing so that I can show the world what I see." Thinking like someone who draws is easy. In fact, you already do it all the time.

- When you see an image or idea and you flip it around in your mind's eye, you're already drawing—just without the paper and pen.
- When you look at a problem with great attention and see the pieces that make it up, you're drawing.

- When you look at a puzzle and see how the pieces fit together, you're drawing.
- When you look at a situation and see what's missing, you're drawing.
- When you gesture while talking to help show what you mean, you're drawing.

Just keep doing those same things but with one difference: Put a pen on paper and start moving the pen—and now you're really drawing.

Here's the best news: While it took you years to learn to write, it only takes a few minutes to learn to draw. (And I'll show you exactly how in Chapter 3.)

How to Start Drawing without Needing to Draw

There are many easy ways to start drawing without becoming self-conscious about it.

Start with a chart. For most businesspeople, making a chart isn't intimidating. Open your spreadsheet, pick a chart template, and select your data. Presto: A chart appears—and you're being visual.

Sketch the sequence. Businesspeople are usually pretty good at process, and processes are often pretty easy to draw. Write down the steps, put them in the correct sequence, and then draw arrows connecting them. Now you've got a picture of what needs to happen and in what order.

Carve the arc. A powerful visual exercise is finding the "through line" that connects many different ideas. Collect a bunch of random but related thoughts (Post-it notes are ideal for this) and stick them up on the wall. Look for common categories and rearrange them into clumps of similar types. Rearrange the complete clumps into a linear sequence from beginning to end. Then draw a single line through the clumps. That line will provide a visual guide for any further discussion.

Capture the emoticon. Emoticons are visual, easy, powerful—and increasingly accepted as a valid communication tool. So rather than drawing anything for your next meeting, simply turn on your smartphone, select an emoticon library, and send yourself a message. Take a screenshot and embed it in your presentation. Look at that: a purely visual story.

The Business Break-Line: A Simple Exercise to Get You Drawing

Here's a quick and easy exercise to get you thinking visually about your own business. I call this the "business break-line." It is a simple illustration of one of the underlying rules of modern business: *Nothing stays the same for long.*

The idea is this: Draw a line that represents the fundamentals of your business. It could be anything—*We sell books, We plan weddings, We build ERP systems, We loan money to homebuyers*; anything at all—whatever is the core of your business.

Then draw a dotted line moving forward. This represents an idea that you, like most everyone else, innately believe: What you do today is probably what you're going to do tomorrow.

The business break-line represents the shake-up of reality ahead. It is a break in the line that appears when someone new steps into your business and messes everything up. Maybe someone invents a new technology, maybe a competitor enters from a completely different field, maybe someone creates an entirely new business model; the break happens when disruption occurs.

The future you predicted is no longer the future ahead—and for many businesses, that's the beginning of the end.

If you think this isn't real, look at these business break-lines from the past couple of years:

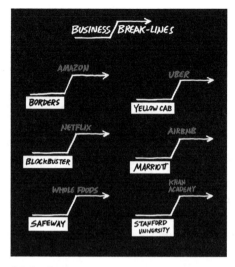

Can you think of more?

Then there's you. Whatever your business is—food, health care, clothing, finance, technology—draw your business line. Then draw a break, and ask yourself, "What might do this to me?"

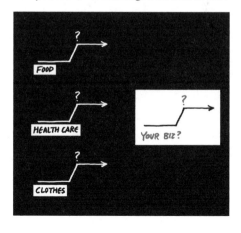

Drawing Is Thinking

We're always looking, but we never really see. When you draw an object, the mind becomes deeply, intensely attentive.

—MILTON GLASER

Stop thinking about drawing as an artistic process. Drawing is a thinking process. If you want to think more clearly about an idea, draw it. If you want to be a more effective leader, think about how you might draw your vision so that other people see it as clearly as you do. If you want to innovate, think about how drawing might help you look at usual things in unusual ways. If you want to sell more, think about how pictures will make your offerings and ideas more compelling than those that aren't visual.

The conversation today is visual. Draw like your world depends on it.

Chapter Checklist

❑ Our world is increasingly about data and data is increasingly visual; to stay relevant and connected, you must embrace our visual capabilities.

❑ Drawing is our oldest technology. Now it has come back with a vengeance.

❑ Drawing isn't an artistic process; drawing is a thinking process.

❑ There are many ways to reengage your visual mind that don't require any drawing at all.

TAKEAWAY: *Today's conversation is visual. To join that conversation, you need to be more visual too.*

CHAPTER 2

WHOEVER DRAWS THE BEST PICTURE WINS

I don't think there is any race driver that could really tell you why he races. But I think he could probably show you.

—STEVE MCQUEEN

Business Has Always Been Visual

In your business, you can no longer afford *not* to be visual. Our visually driven world now demands that pictures step to the front. But this is not a new phenomenon; pictures have always been at the heart of great breakthroughs in science, economics, technology, politics, and business. What is new is that you can't ignore the visual anymore. And that's a good thing.

Why? Because there is a simple unwritten rule about the power of pictures that you can always rely on: *Whoever draws the best picture wins.*

What It Means to Win

In business, *winning* is a pretty straightforward formula: You find something that you can do well enough to earn enough money to keep doing it. That's the business cycle: Do something other people want (if you're lucky, it's something you also love to do), find a way to sell it to them, keep improving how you do it, and train someone else so that they can do it when you're gone. There are a million variations, but that's the basic theme.

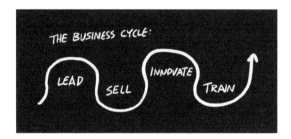

No matter what your business does, these four tasks keep you driving forward: You must **lead**, you must **sell**, you must **innovate**, and you must **train**. Do all four well and your business will win for a long time; miss any of the four and sooner or later your business will stop.

But just because the formula is simple doesn't mean it's easy. There are an infinite number of ways to lead, sell, innovate, and train. The beauty of pictures is that they help clarify and streamline all four tasks.

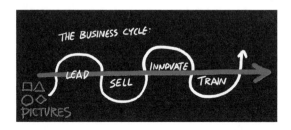

1. **Lead:** Pictures help you clarify your vision and share it so that other people see where you want to go.
2. **Sell:** Pictures help you deeply understand a problem and then show other people that you have a way to solve it.
3. **Innovate:** Pictures help you look at the same old things in new ways—and then find ways to make those old things undeniably better.
4. **Train:** Pictures help you map out the steps of what you do so that you can show other people how they can do it too.

So here's this chapter's rule again, only this time with its mercenary subtext:

Whoever best describes the problem, solution, or idea will be the best understood.

And . . .

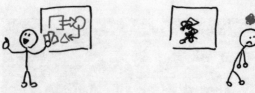

Whoever draws the best picture gets the funding.

That's the essence of this chapter: If you're truly serious about solving your problem, selling your solution, or explaining your idea—let's be blunt: *if you want your project or business to get funded*—the best way is to provide the clearest picture of what you're trying to say. It really is as simple as that: If you draw the best explanation of an idea, you will win. Why? Because when you see something that makes sense to you, it lodges in your brain and activates your memory in a way that words never will.

From Whiteboard to White House

If it's a good movie, the sound could go off and the audience would still have a perfectly clear idea of what was going on.

—ALFRED HITCHCOCK

Here is the story of how pictures helped me win in an industry in which I didn't even know I had a role: health care.

In 2008, health care in America got ugly. The president proposed sweeping changes to the American health care system and in response the country started to tear itself apart. Depending on which news service you paid attention to, "Obamacare" was either (A) the greatest positive transformation of social services in the history of the country or (B) the most heinous plot to destroy the nation ever devised. Pick A or B. There really was no other option.

I didn't know enough about health care in America to have a well-formed opinion one way or the other. But when I turned on the news and saw people arriving at town hall meetings bringing guns and getting in fistfights, I knew two things: First, I'd better stop watching the news, and second, I'd better start figuring out what the debate was really all about. Which meant I'd better start drawing some pictures.

As a consultant, I'd had an opportunity to work with a handful of important health care organizations, but I knew I was no expert. So I contacted a consultant friend named Tony (an MD and former colleague with deep health care expertise) and, with printouts of the actual health care law in hand, we locked ourselves in an office full of whiteboards and agreed not to leave until we'd come up with a series of simple drawings that explained the thinking behind the law.

Two days later, Tony and I emerged with forty-three drawings in hand. I put the drawings into a PowerPoint, added headlines and a single-sentence narration to each page, and posted it online. Within a week we had a thousand downloads. Within a month we had fifty thousand. As of today, our "American Health Care: A 4-Napkin Explanation" has been downloaded more than 2.1 million times, was featured on the *Huffington Post* and countless other websites, and was awarded the title "World's Best Presentation of 2009" by SlideShare. But that's not the *win* I wanted to share. Because what happened next still rocks my world.

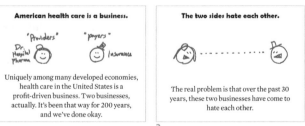

American health care is a business.

"Providers"
Dr.
Hospital
Pharma

"payers"
Insurance

Uniquely among many developed economies, health care in the United States is a profit-driven business. Two businesses, actually. It's been that way for 200 years, and we've done okay.

1

The two sides hate each other.

The real problem is that over the past 30 years, these two businesses have come to hate each other.

2

We're in the middle.

We're the only source of money going into the system.

3

We're getting squeezed.

As both sides rightfully seek to maximize their profit, we are the ones who get financially squeezed.

4

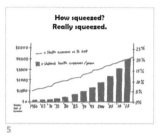

How squeezed? Really squeezed.

5

Government wants to help...

This administration looked at the balance, and thought that the best place to start was the 'payer' side.

6

About a month after I'd posted the presentation, I got a call from Fox News in New York. "Dan," said the producer on the phone, "since you are clearly one of America's leading thinkers on health care reform, would you be willing to come on air and use your pictures to explain to our viewers what the law actually says?"

"I'd be delighted," I replied. (Keep in mind that I live in San Francisco, a city that I'm pretty sure sends out an electromagnetic pulse to block Fox News airwaves from even entering the city.) A week later, I recorded a seven-minute live segment with the Fox Business Network, walking through the first ten drawings. It was a breakthrough for me: Not only did my business *win* national television exposure, more important, millions of viewers saw a new and clearer way of thinking about the debate.

But that's still not the end of the story.

A week after my Fox appearance, I got another call. The voice on the other end of the line asked, "Is this the Dan Roam who was on Fox showing pictures of health care?"

"Yes," I replied, wondering what this was all about.

"This is the White House Office of Communications. We wondered if you might be willing to come to Washington, DC, and share your visual process with the president's online communications staff." I said yes and I went. Twice.

So here's the question: Am I America's leading expert on health care reform? Absolutely not. But am I the guy asked to explain it on national TV and at the White House? Yes. Why? Because I was the guy who *drew* it. Remember: *Whoever draws the best picture wins.*

But What If You Can't Draw?

If this all sounds great but still seems out of reach—because, well, *you can't draw*—there is something else to remember: *Drawing isn't an artistic process; drawing is a thinking process.* What drawing does is help you think in a way that is more exploratory, expansive, and connective—and faster, usually *much faster*—than writing.

So don't worry: Lots of the most successful people in business, science, leadership, and even entertainment discovered the power of pictures when they needed a breakthrough—and they weren't artists either.

SOUTHWEST AIRLINES

The year is 1967. Two business guys are sitting in the bar of the St. Anthony Club in San Antonio, Texas. Rollin King draws a triangle on a napkin. Herb Kelleher likes it. They agree to start Southwest Airlines, which goes on to become the most successful airline in history. (That napkin is now featured in the "History" section of Southwest's website.)

THE LAFFER CURVE

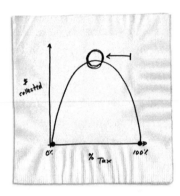

It's 1974, and President Ford needs to rethink taxation as a part of his economic recovery program. He asks University of Chicago economist Arthur Laffer to consult with his cabinet. One night at dinner with Ford's chiefs of staff, Donald Rumsfeld and Dick Cheney (later George W. Bush's secretary of defense and vice president), Laffer draws his new tax concept on a cocktail napkin—a napkin that inspires President Reagan to turn traditional economics on its head and create Reaganomics. (That napkin is now on display at the Smithsonian Institution in Washington, DC.)

EGO, SUPEREGO, AND ID

By 1933, Sigmund Freud's general model of the human subconscious is complete. In one of his last papers, he seeks to clarify the relationship between those parts of our minds to which we have conscious access and those that remain hidden. To illustrate these various layers—what Freud calls the *Ego*, the *Superego*, and the *Id*—he sketches a simple diagram. It is published in Freud's *New Introductory Lectures on Psycho-Analysis*, and for the first time, students of psychology see clearly what Freud has been alluding to for years.

HEDY LAMARR'S TORPEDOES

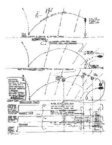

Speaking of Freud, Hollywood's most glamorous leading lady of the early 1940s is deeply intrigued by torpedoes and the means to control them. Working with her Hollywood neighbor and composer

George Antheil, Hedy Lamarr (real name Hedwig Eva Maria Kiesler), sets up a drafting room in her bungalow and draws out plans for frequency hopping in acoustic torpedo guidance. In 1942, she and Antheil are awarded US Patent 2,292,387, elements of which eventually make their way into the earliest versions of the World Wide Web.

DONELLA MEADOWS AND MIT

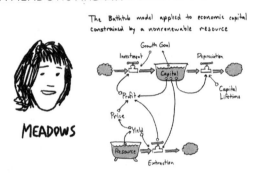

MEADOWS

The Bathtub model applied to economic capital constrained by a nonrenewable resource

In 1971, Donella Meadows, a biophysics PhD from Harvard, joins the MIT team working on systems dynamics. To more deeply understand the relationships governing resource flow in complex systems, Donella draws a sketch of a bathtub. Then she adds inlets and drains, reservoirs and bypass valves. Before long, her sketching becomes the core of her team's work and the basis for the computer models they build. *Thinking in Systems* is born and Donella wins a MacArthur Fellows "Genius Grant" for her contributions to environmental science.

HARRY POTTER

A single mother on welfare sits in a café sketching maps and time-lines illustrating the many characters, locations, and adventures that intersect in the life of a young wizard she has conjured up in her imagination. She writes out the stories on a manual typewriter and submits the manuscript—without the pictures—to many publishers. All reject her story. Finally one bites, and J. K. Rowling goes on to become the second wealthiest woman in the UK, after the Queen. Only later, after her literary reputation is unshakable, does she share the drawings made years before. When J. K. Rowling hand draws a limited edition copy of *The Tales of Beedle the Bard*, it sells for $3.98 million at auction.

The List of Winners Who Draw Is a Long List

Once you start looking, these examples are countless. From Leonardo da Vinci to Alexander Graham Bell, from Thomas Edison to Steve Jobs, from Charles Schwab to Sir Richard Branson, all of these undeniably successful winners in technology, finance, and business have at least one thing in common: They *drew.*

But Is It Real?

I started drawing in business a long time ago. And I learned something almost immediately: Whenever our team went into a business pitch with an insightful picture already prepared and ready to show the client, we won the engagement. Every single time.

That Goes for Big Wins . . .

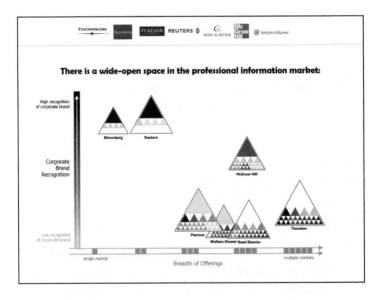

We were asked by Thomson, a major business publisher preparing to list on NYSE, to do a brand survey presentation for a few thousand dollars. Along the way we discovered some interesting insights about the industry, which we captured in a series of charts. When the CEO saw the charts, he had a strategic insight that got him so excited he ended up awarding us more than $4 million in consulting work—and led his company to ultimately acquire Reuters, forming Thomson Reuters, the largest professional publishing company on earth.

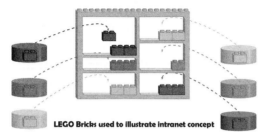

LEGO Bricks used to illustrate intranet concept

We pitched the chief technology officer of McKinsey & Company on a novel approach to create a knowledge-management portal. We illustrated our thinking with LEGO bricks and drawings. We won the engagement, even though we were the smallest and least experienced company bidding for the job.

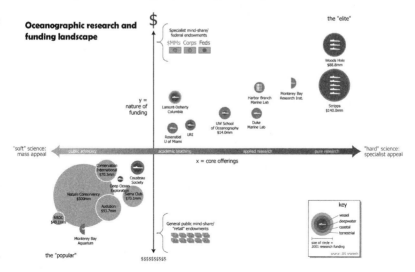

In a competitive bid for strategy work for the Woods Hole Oceanographic Institute (the people who found the *Titanic*, discovered deep-water currents, and know more about climate change than anyone else on earth), we created a visual "map of the science market" that surfaced old data in a new way. When the director of the institute saw the visual, he canceled further competitive presentations, saying, "You've already shown me exactly what I'm looking for." Our team got to spend that summer on Cape Cod doing the project.

. . . And for Small Wins

What goes for big fish goes for the smaller ones as well.

Method for forced containment of deep water oil leak

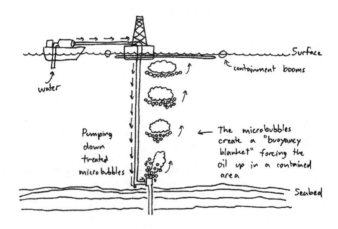

During the Deepwater Horizon oil spill in the Gulf of Mexico, I drew simple, cartoonlike pictures for a small Louisiana-based oil field company with a big idea about how to contain the oil. The company wasn't attracting the interest of federal and state agencies, which were overwhelmed by the disaster. But when our pictures got in front of local authorities, word spread fast. Soon, this new technology was deployed and helped make a difference in cleaning up the spill.

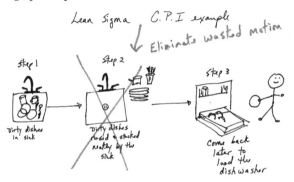

Two years ago, a friend lost her IT project manager job. We worked together to create a series of simple pictures that helped her think through her own career goals and redefine her capabilities. She used the sketches as a road map for finding a better position—and then used more detailed pictures to show her potential employer why she was the only real candidate. She got the job. (And at higher pay than they were originally offering.)

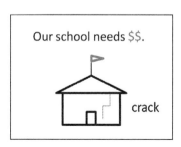

And last, my daughter's school needed additional funding for minor building repairs. I created a simple set of drawings to illustrate the need to parents. Response was better than expected, and the money came in.

I really mean it: *Whoever draws the best picture wins.*

The Pen-Color Test

You might not draw the way I do, or the way Hedy or Steve Jobs did. You might not even draw at all. But you are still *visual*. The key is recognizing your visual strengths and putting your visual mind to work.

The Pen Color Self-Assessment Exercise

Years ago, I created a quick self-assessment exercise to help people find their visual-thinking strengths. The spectrum runs from "Black Pen" people (people who draw out their ideas all the time) to "Yellow Pen" (people who rarely draw but find it interesting to look at visuals) to "Red Pen" (people who never draw and prefer detailed text descriptions).

After running the assessment in four-hundred-plus live meetings including well over fifty thousand participants, the results are consistent: 25 percent of us draw a lot, 50 percent draw a little, and 25 percent don't draw at all. We all fall across a bell-curve distribution that looks like the chart below. Go ahead and take the assessment and see where you fall on the curve.

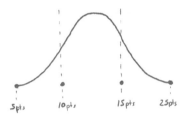

5 pts   10 pts   15 pts   25 pts

THE "WHICH COLOR IS YOUR PEN?" ASSESSMENT

SELECT THE SINGLE BEST ANSWER FOR EACH OF THE QUESTIONS BELOW.

A. **I'm in a brainstorming session in a conference room that has a big whiteboard. I want to . . .**

   1. Go to the board and start drawing circles and boxes.

   2. Go to the board and start writing categorized lists.

   3. Add something to clarify what's already up there.

   4. Forget the whiteboard—we've got work to do!

   5. I hate brainstorming sessions.

B. **Someone hands me a pen and asks me to sketch out a particular idea. I . . .**

   1. Ask for more pens—in at least three colors.

   2. Just start sketching and see what emerges.

3. Say, "I can't draw, but . . ." and make something ugly.

4. Write a few words, then put boxes around them.

5. Put the pen on the table and start talking.

C. **Someone hands me a complex, multipage spreadsheet table printout. I first . . .**

1. Glaze over and hope it will go away.

2. Flip through and see if anything interesting just pops up.

3. Read across the column headers to identify categories.

4. Look for common data results across multiple cells.

5. Notice that OPEX variance to budget is down for the second quarter.

D. **On my way home from a conference, I run into a colleague at the airport bar, and he or she asks me what I do. I . . .**

1. Grab a napkin and ask the waiter for a pen.

2. Build an organizational chart with packs of sugar.

3. Pull a PowerPoint page out of my carry-on.

4. Say, "Better buy another round—this takes a while."

5. Shift the conversation to something more interesting.

E. **If I were an astronaut floating in space, the first thing I would do is:**

1. Take a deep breath and take in the whole view.

2. Pull out my camera.

3. Start describing what I see.

4. Close my eyes.

5. Find a way to get back into my spacecraft.

NOW ADD UP YOUR TOTAL SCORE TO RATE YOURSELF.

SCORE	CALCULATED PEN PREFERENCE
5–9	Hand me the pen! (Black Pen)
10–14	I can't draw, but . . . (Yellow Pen)
15+	I'm not visual. (Red Pen)

Where did you come in? Whether your pen color is Black, Yellow, or Red matters because it helps guide where you want to focus your visual energies. If you're a Black Pen, the next chapter will be a no-brainer for you. If you're a Yellow Pen, the next chapter will get you drawing more. And if you're a Red Pen, the next chapter will show you exactly how to kick your visual-thinking engine into gear—with no sweat.

Chapter Checklist

❑ Pictures help you win. Simple pictures offer a proven way to help you lead, sell, innovate, and train.

❑ You don't need to be an artist to create pictures. Many of the greatest ideas in business, science, politics, and literature have been *drawn* by people with no formal artistic skills.

❑ Not everyone is an artist, but everyone is visual. You occupy your own personal niche on the spectrum of visual problem-solving. Find it and embrace it.

TAKEAWAY: *Your visual mind is a great friend; learn to use it and you will succeed in ways you never expected.*

CHAPTER 3

FIRST DRAW A CIRCLE, THEN GIVE IT A NAME

The way to get started is to quit talking and begin doing.

—WALT DISNEY

First Off, Drawing Is Not Art; Drawing Is Thinking

If I can't picture it, I can't understand it.

—ALBERT EINSTEIN

This chapter will not show you how to draw like a talented artist; this chapter will show you how to draw like a clear thinker. If you think you can't draw, you'll see that you're mistaken. You can draw; you just need to learn two simple tools, see them in action, and then practice using them a couple of times.

That's all it takes. Make the analogy to talking. The first time you tried to talk, you didn't do very well. But with tools, training, and practice, you got good at it. It's the same here; just as you don't need to be a novelist to talk, you don't need to be an artist to be visual.

Drawing the First Line Is the Hardest— So Don't Even Think About It

The one time in drawing when you *don't think* is when you draw the first line. Because the first line is the hardest, you really should tell your mind to quiet down—and then put your pen on your paper and draw a circle.

❑ Draw a circle. Your drawing is started.

Then, kick your brain back into gear by thinking up a name for that circle. You can call it almost anything, whatever is at the top of your mind as you approach the idea you want to convey: *me, you, today, tomorrow, profit, our product, my company, the globe.* As long as you call it something, your thought process has started.

❑ Give your circle a name. Write it in the circle.

Now your thinking has started too.

HOW TO START A DRAWING

Once You've Drawn the First Circle, the Next Is Easy

Add a few more shapes beside your first circle—a square, a triangle, and a star. Now connect them with arrows. Now label them; like magic, you've created a schematic diagram of an idea.

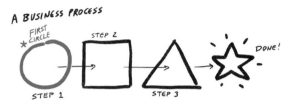

Most of the time, the simple act of drawing the first circle and naming it is all you need to get started. Then just continue the process. Almost always, one drawing leads to another, which leads to another.

Keep Adding (and Naming) Circles, and You Can Draw All Kinds of Ideas

Look for the first circles in the drawings below. Do you see how many different ideas you can express just by adding more circles, more labels, and a few details?

First-circle drawing 1. Three intersecting circles become a Venn diagram that illustrates the overlap of three components of an idea; in this case how to make a perfect cup of coffee. (The same drawing might illustrate your business offerings, your customer segments, or your marketing plan.)

First-circle drawing 2. Three circles with simple faces become an insightful **map** of a competitive landscape; in this case the eternal triangle of human heartbreak. (The same drawing might illustrate your competitive positioning, your customer acquisition approach, or your hiring needs.)

First-circle drawing 3. Two big circles, two small circles, and a triangle become a bicycle—or any number of other **objects**. (Similar drawings might illustrate your product offering or your go-to-market plan.)

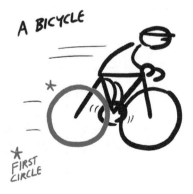

Once You've Started Drawing, the Hardest Part Soon Becomes Stopping

Because so many drawings can emerge from that first circle, once you've got one circle drawn, the others keep coming. Before you know it, you've drawn boxes and triangles, lines and arrows—and the idea that was buried in your head now takes shape before your eyes.

In fact, once you've started drawing, the hardest thing is stopping. That's the power of our visual mind; once on a roll, watch out: Ideas are going to flow. This simplest of triggers—a circle with a name—is all you need to kick your visual mind into gear.

And if you do get stuck, you can always reignite your visual mind by spicing up your picture with new shapes, new arrows, and new labels.

Drawing Is Easy When You Start with the Basic Shapes

Ninety percent of all the business pictures you will ever need to create are composed of just seven basic building blocks:

1. Dot
2. Line
3. Arrow
4. Square
5. Triangle
6. Circle
7. Blob

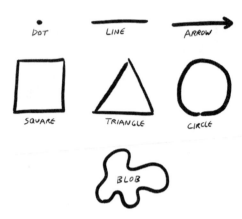

With just these seven shapes, you can draw almost anything.

You Create All the Building Blocks the Same Way: Start by Drawing a Dot—and Then Just Keeping Pushing Your Pen

Drawing is like talking: There is silence until you say something. So say, "Dot," and then draw a dot. The way you *talk visually* is by holding your pen on that dot and then drawing a line in the appropriate direction.

Which direction is appropriate? That depends on the basic shape you want to draw.

TOOL 3A: THE SEVEN BASIC BUILDING-BLOCK SHAPES

Here is how to draw the seven basic building-block shapes:

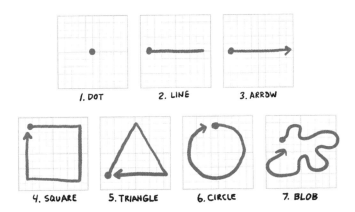

1. **Dot**. The starting point for all lines.
2. **Line**. The starting line for all shapes.
3. **Arrow.** A line that indicates direction, influence, or transition.
4. **Square.** Four dots connected by four lines. By lengthening lines, you create a rectangle. By skewing lines, you create a trapezoid.
5. **Triangle**. Three dots connected by three lines. By lengthening lines, you can create any three-sided shape.
6. **Circle**. A line that chases its own tail. By squeezing the circle, you create ovals.
7. **Blob**. A line that wanders before coming back home. The blob represents things that are unstructured—and perhaps problematic.

Every Picture You're Going to Create in Business Is a Combination of These Simple Shapes

To create more meaningful pictures, you simply combine these seven building blocks. The combinations are pretty easy too; there are just six essential business pictures that illustrate and explain almost every idea you will explore.

You Can Create Most Basic Objects by Combining the Shapes and Then Erasing the Hidden Lines

1. You create simple **objects and people** by combining squares, circles, and triangles.
2. You draw a **chart** by stacking rectangles or slicing up a circle.
3. You create a **map** by crossing two arrows and placing shapes in the appropriate quadrants.
4. You create a **timeline** by lining up big, thick arrows (which are rectangles paired with pointy triangles) in a row.
5. You can create elaborate **flowcharts** by sorting shapes into order and linking them with arrows.
6. You can create **equations** by combining any number of your simple shapes.

Practice making these six pictures by combining your basic shapes. Being able to draw just these will account for 90 percent of all the business drawings you will ever need.

TOOL 3B: BUILDING-BLOCK COMBINATIONS THAT CREATE THE SIX ESSENTIAL BUSINESS PICTURES

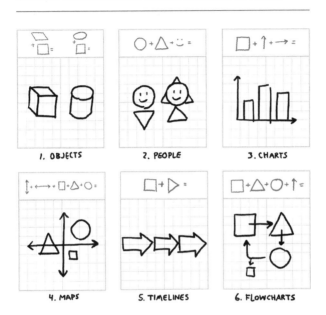

1. OBJECTS	*2.* PEOPLE	*3.* CHARTS
4. MAPS	*5.* TIMELINES	*6.* FLOWCHARTS

It Is Easier to Draw Something Complex by Building up Shapes Than It Is to Draw the Whole Thing at Once

The biggest mistake you can make in business visualization is to expect that you can quickly draw your entire idea as a single finished picture. With practice, that might become an admirable goal, but at the beginning it's a damagingly unrealistic expectation. You won't get far and will probably give up before you have seen the thought-clarifying power of pictures.

Instead, start by drawing just part of your idea. Using one of the simple building-block shapes, sketch out a single element and give it a name. Then ask yourself, "What might come next?" Draw out that second part and give it a name as well. Keep going. Once just a few parts are visible on paper, your visual mind will take over.

As it sees the connections and relationships emerging, your visual mind will begin to expand rapidly, circling things, detecting new possibilities, and adding elements. *You want this to happen*; this is where you begin to detect patterns and expose ideas that were invisible when you were just talking.

Take the Boeing 787 Dreamliner for example. This advanced aircraft is considered the most complex machine to ever be mass-produced. How does Boeing work with six hundred direct suppliers speaking fourteen different languages to build it? Two ways: First, all communications are picture-based; second, those drawings break the entire machine down into components, drawing it out piece by piece. Apply the same thinking to your business idea and watch it make sense.

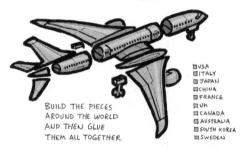

HOW TO BUILD A DREAMLINER:

BUILD THE PIECES
AROUND THE WORLD
AND THEN GLUE
THEM ALL TOGETHER.

USA
ITALY
JAPAN
CHINA
FRANCE
UK
CANADA
AUSTRALIA
SOUTH KOREA
SWEDEN

A Brief Aside on Analytic versus Synthetic Drawing

There is a technical term for this piece-by-piece drawing approach. In academic circles, it is called analytic or reductionist drawing, in which you see an idea or object as a collection of distinct parts. Because it helps you break complexity down into individually understandable elements, this is the better approach 90 percent of the time for your visual business problem-solving.

On the other side is synthetic or gestalt drawing, in which you strive to capture the entire idea as one seamless object. This is a good approach for trying to see the whole, but is rarely useful for "working the problem." Plus, for most people, it is a lot harder to draw anything this way—and leads to exactly the frustration that makes most people give up before they have explored drawing's amazing potential.

ANALYTIC HORSE

This is the kind of drawing you want to make: step-by-step, working from individual parts up to the whole.

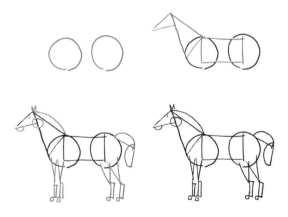

GESTALT HORSE

Trying to draw this kind of picture will frustrate you: Trying to see and capture an entire idea all at once ususally does not help see how it is constructed.

In Drawing, You Mostly Just Need to Get out of Your Own Way

Once I am in the square circle, I am in my home.

—FLOYD MAYWEATHER JR.

Things That Make Drawing Hard
- Impatience
- Wondering what to draw
- Worrying about what's next
- Editing as you go
- A blank sheet
- "Art"

Things That Make Drawing Easy
- Curiosity
- Starting with a circle

- Letting your hand go
- Drawing now, editing later
- Making marks on the page
- "Just do it"

Basic Business Drawing Example: What Does *Innovation* Look Like? (And Why Should We Care?)

Working in Silicon Valley, you hear a lot about *innovation*: "We need to innovate this," and "We'll innovate our way to a solution." But it's rare you hear "*Why* innovate?" (I mean, what's wrong with doing the same thing over and over? Isn't that how you get good at it?)

Here is a simple example of how drawing things out helps to answer a big question like "Why innovate?"

WHY INNOVATE ?

BECAUSE ...

$$\square + \triangle = \bigcirc$$

- This **square** represents how we do things today. We know our business well and we have optimized everything we can. (*Our corners are square and our lines are straight.*)
- This **triangle** represents *change*; it serves as a reminder that we work in a world that is constantly revolving. How big is this triangle? That depends on the business we're in.

- This **circle** represents what we're going to look like *on the other side* of the change. Will we look completely different? Or will we just round things off a bit?

This simple little picture—which you can draw in about fifteen seconds—gives you hours of ideas you can discuss with your client, customer, or team:

- How well do we know our business today?
- How big—and how fast—is change coming in our industry?
- What might we look like on the other side of that change?

That's the power of starting with a circle and pushing on. When broken down into visual building blocks, even complex business ideas can become clear.

Chapter Checklist

- ☐ Drawing is not art; drawing is thinking.
- ☐ To start drawing, make a circle and give it a name.
- ☐ There are seven basic building-block shapes: **dot, line, arrow, square, triangle, circle,** and **blob.** They are all easy to draw.
- ☐ Practice the simple shapes and combine them to create the six essential business pictures: **objects and people, charts, maps, timelines, flowcharts,** and **equations.**

TAKEAWAY: *Anyone can become more visual; we need only pick up a pen, draw a circle, give it a name—and then keep going.*

CHAPTER 4

LEAD WITH THE EYE AND THE MIND WILL FOLLOW

More of the brain is dedicated to processing vision than to any other known function.

—DR. LEO CHALUPA

You Are a Magnificent Visualist

Forget for a moment about whether you can draw or not. Think about this instead:

1. More of your brain is dedicated to processing vision than to any other thing that you do.

Recent estimates from the visual neurosciences indicate that vision likely accounts for close to two-thirds of your total brain activity. Roughly one-third of your brain's neurons are dedicated to visual processing and another third are occupied by vision combined with other sensory processing. That leaves one-third of your brain for everything else.

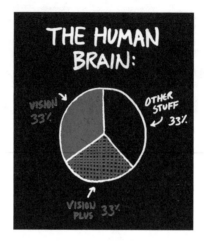

2. Your brain consumes more energy than any other organ in your body.

The average American weighs 196 pounds. The average human brain weighs 3 pounds, or less than 2 percent of the body's total weight. Yet your brain consumes 20 percent of your total calorie burn every day.

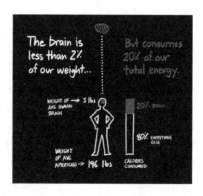

In other words, more of your brain is occupied with *seeing* than with anything else, and your brain consumes more energy than *anything else in your body*. As far as your body is concerned, seeing is measure for measure the most important thing you do.

Where Does All That Vision Go?

Clearly, being able to see is important. Vision guides you, protects you, excites you, and teaches you. In sheer neurological numbers, vision outweighs all your other senses combined. And the coolest thing of all? You're not even aware of it. You never notice how hard your vision system is working just to keep you upright and moving. What's miraculous is how hands-off and reliable vision is.

The simple neurobiological fact is that your eyes love to look. Color, shape, size, texture, position, pattern; your eyes marvel at all the stuff there is out there to see. Your eyes love looking because, above all else, your eyes love trying to figure stuff out—and they are really good at it.

Just imagine what you could do with all that horsepower in your visual system if you had a better understanding of it how it worked. Well, you can: You can become deeply aware of the power of your visual sense, you can easily understand how vision works, and when you do, you will see why *you can persuade more effectively with pictures than with anything else.* Period.

The Return on Your Visual Investment

Sight costs a lot. Given the investment your brain has in vision, your body demands a high ROI (return on investment) from it. Simply put, if there is nothing interesting for you to look at, your visual engine will simply pack its bags and go in search of greener pastures—and will take most of your attention with it. This is why 90 percent of all PowerPoint presentations fail: because there is nothing to look at other than bulleted text and a talking head (neither of which are visually interesting for more than a couple of minutes). So of course your audience's visual mind leaves; it really has no choice. Two to three minutes of bullet points and *poof!* Your audience is gone and you're wondering why no one is interested in all the amazing ideas you have to share.

So How Do You Keep the Eyes Engaged?

The good news is that you can learn to keep people's eyes focused and engaged for hours—and it's not rocket science. Once you understand how vision functions, you will see that there are several ways to keep the eye engaged, the simplest of which is just to mark things up as you talk. Every time you make a mark, you are saying to the eye, "Hey! Look over here! Isn't this cool? Now look over here. Neat, huh?" It sounds absurdly simple, but it also works 100 percent of the time. Why? Because when you lead with the eye, the rest of the mind will follow. So here's how to do the leading part . . .

THE TOP SEVEN WAYS TO ENGAGE THE EYE

1. Mark up your words as you talk.

2. Draw a picture as you talk. (Or at least show a picture as you talk.)

3. Make sure your picture aligns with your words.

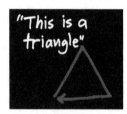

4. Keep your picture simple and focused.

5. If your picture is complex, explain it.

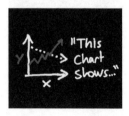

6. If your idea is complex, draw it step-by-step.

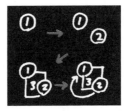

7. Draw the right pictures in the right order.

Now, what are the right pictures and what is the right order? I'm glad you asked.

The Right Order for Thinking Is the Right Order for Drawing

There is a classic journalist's approach to understanding and explaining a concept, and it dates all the way back to the ancient Greeks. Today, we call this approach the Five Ws, and it is still taught as early as in the elementary classroom all the way up through college in top journalism schools.

QUIS, QUID, QUANDO, UBI,
CUR, QUEM AD MODUM,
QUIBUS ADMINICULIS.*

- **Hermagoras of Temnos**
1st Century BC

*Who, what, when, where,
why, in what way,
by what means.*

The idea is this: If you want to understand or explain something, you can be certain that you're covering all the essentials if you include the original Five Ws: *who, what, when, where, why,* plus a sixth called "how much." From a cognitive science perspective, it turns out the Greeks were onto something. Although they didn't know it at the time, they were creating a pretty accurate map of the mind. (Specifically, the neocortex, or "thinking" part of the brain.) In the two thousand years since, we've added only one more "W": *how much,* to account for the fact that your brain likes to *count* things too. The Six Ws are a solid model you can rely on whenever you're writing and want to ensure clarity, comprehensiveness, and comprehension.

But what if I told you there was a way to use this old rule to visually explain your ideas that is even easier? Even better, what if I showed you?

First, You Need to See How Vision Works

(If you want to skip right to the pictures, feel free—although I think understanding how your vision works is actually pretty cool.) From a neuromechanical process perspective, vision works like this:

1. Light bounces off the objects in front of you and, through a kind of instant scan, enters your eyes as photons. But those photons are just little electrical signals and they don't mean anything yet, so your visual engine (your retinas, optic nerves, visual cortex, and about fifty billion neurons) has to kick into gear to make sense of them.

2. Right away, your eyes start filtering those electrical signals and begin to pass them along a series of initial pathways. The What Pathway identifies the objects, the How Much Pathway counts the objects, and the Where Pathway determines the position of the objects. These three pathways are more or less independent, and they operate in parallel throughout physically distinct regions of your brain.

3. By detecting changes in the positions of the objects over *multiple scans*, the When Pathway captures the sequence in which the objects are interacting. This gives your mind the impression that things are moving, or to put it more practically, that time is passing.

4. The How Pathway (the highest level of visual processing) pulls everything together—the objects, their numbers and positions, and the sequence in which they occur—and creates a kind of visual cause-and-effect model, through which it tells the rest of your brain what is happening in the visible world around you.

5. Last, the Why Pathway (which really isn't so much a pathway as it is *visual cognition*) takes that cause-and-effect story and makes rules from it; a kind of "news you can use." The whole process from photon to insight takes about one-tenth of a second, and happens constantly as long as your eyes are open. (It also takes place when you are dreaming, but that's another story.) Along the way, the visual inputs merge with those from your other senses to give you the complete sensory picture.

This is a simplified schematic of how vision works:

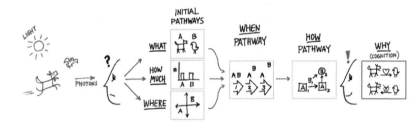

There are two things this process tells you that are critical. First, vision isn't random; the system relies on the *same kinds of pictures* delivered in the *same order* over and over and over again. Second, vision is *predictable*. Understand these two facts and you've got an unbeatably powerful way to repeatedly and predictably lead the eye and, thus, lead the mind—and all with the simplest of pictures.

You Need Only Six Pictures to Explain Anything— Your Vision Isn't Random

There is another way of drawing that same schematic diagram of vision. This time, don't worry about what the brain does; just look at what it sees. This simplified version shows the six types of pictures the brain is looking for:

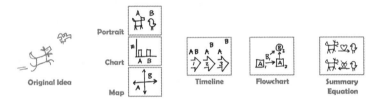

This matters because it tells you that if you can draw six simple pictures—**portrait (of people or objects), chart, map, timeline, flowchart,** and **equation**—you can visually clarify and explain anything.

Now you see why I walked you through the step-by-step creation of the six essential business pictures (Tool 3B) in the previous chapter. These images aren't just good building blocks for more advanced pictures; they *are* the advanced pictures. As you seek visual clarity in your own thinking and seek to present clear visuals to others, these six pictures are all you really need to know.

TOOL 4A: THE SIX ESSENTIAL PICTURES OF VISUAL EXPLANATION

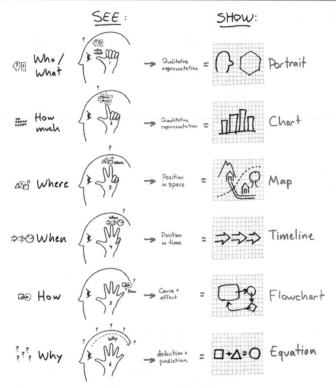

Vision Is Predictable

The second great insight we've learned about the visual process is that vision is predictable. What this means in practice is that at any point during your problem-solving, presentation, lesson, or explanation, you can reliably and accurately predict exactly what your audience's visual system is looking for. And if you give your audience the right pictures in the right order, you can use those pictures to:

- Explain anything.
- Make anything memorable.
- Make anything magnetic.

"Wow" is right. Even things you think you knew take on a different meaning, depth, and clarity when you see them drawn with the six pictures.

Your Executive Committee of Vision

Think about your vision system as a well-run business. Vision is like an effective executive team sitting in your brain. This team keeps you alive, safe, and thriving by helping you see the world around you and navigate its hazards.

Like many big businesses, your visual executive team has six members, each of whom is responsible for managing one of your six visual pathways. Your chief marketing officer takes care of your What Pathway, your chief financial officer handles How Much, your chief strategy officer monitors Where, your chief operations officer takes care of When, your chief technology officer handles How, and your CEO is responsible for Why.

In this business of *sight*, each of your executives is responsible for collecting a specific type of visual information and for using that to create a specific picture to share with the rest of the team.

Here is each executive's pictorial responsibility:

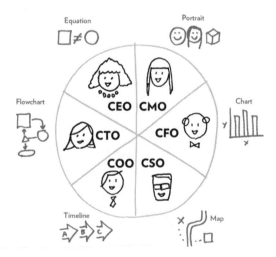

Here is the order in which each executive collects and reports his or her part of the visual story.

I'm the **CMO**.
Let me show you WHO our customers are and WHAT we offer them.
(*I draw the* **Portrait**.)

1. Your visual chief marketing officer draws the portrait.

First up is your CMO. She is the one who needs to figure out *who* the people in the audience are and identify *what* all the things are around you. Do you know them? Do they impact you? What do they want from you?

The CMO draws the portrait that shows "These are the people and these are the things. So . . . what are we going to do about it?"

I'm the **CFO**.
Let me show you HOW MUCH we have and how much we need.
(*I draw the* **Chart**.)

2. Your chief financial officer draws the chart.

The CFO is your vision system's accountant. First, he has to counts things to get a good sense of the numbers: *How much is out there?* Then, he has to note the trends: *Are the quantities increasing or decreasing?*

The CFO draws the chart that shows these numbers and trends—and how they might impact you and the rest of the team.

I'm the **CSO**.
Let me show you
WHERE we are now and
where we are going.
(I draw the Map.)

3. Your chief strategy officer draws the map.

Meanwhile, your CSO is noting the position of everything; what is close (*Worry about this now!*), what is far (*Worry about it later*), and where the open spaces are (*Let's go there!*).

Constantly identifying positional risk and seeking new chances for success, your CSO draws the map that captures the location of threats and opportunities. If his map is accurate, you and the team know where to look next.

I'm the **COO**.
Let me show you
WHEN we are taking
each step along the way.
(I draw the Timeline.)

4. Your chief operations officer draws the timeline.

The COO brings the portraits, charts, and maps into sequential alignment, making sure that the order is correct and that timing overlaps are accurate.

With this information, he then draws the timeline that shows what has happened leading up to this moment and what you need to do next in order to keep things moving along. Great; you and the team now have next-step marching orders.

I'm the **CTO**.
Let me show you HOW
we are technologically
making this all happen.
(*I draw the **Flowchart**.*)

5. Your chief technical officer draws the flowchart.

The inputs are clear, the numbers are there, and the process is mapped. What remains? Building the systems and architecture that makes taking the next steps technologically feasible. That's the job of the CTO.

The picture she draws? The flowchart; it shows how the pieces interact, how the information flows, and how to monitor all the incoming data. It's usually the most complex picture, so it demands exceptional attention to logic and clarity.

I'm the **CEO**.
Let me show you
WHY we're doing
what we're doing.
(*I draw the **Equation**.*)

6. Your chief executive officer draws the visual equation.

As the ultimate leader of the organization, the CEO has to look at all the inputs and make the final decisions as to what you will do next.

The best way the CEO can show *why* she has made the decisions she has is by showing a simple "visual equation."

Think of this as the moral of the story made visual, the simplest possible visual that says the most in the clearest possible way, giving you and your full team vision, direction, and purpose.

That's it: Those are the roles your visual executives play, those are the pictures they draw, and that's the order in which they present them to your brain. When you understand that sequence, you can mirror it in your visual processing and, as you'll see in the following chapters, let it guide you to effective visual decision-making.

Chapter Checklist

❑ We are all magnificently visual; more of your daily energy burn goes to looking at the world than to anything else.

❑ When you understand how vision works, you can hijack the process to inspire, motivate, and guide other people.

❑ Vision is predictable. When you draw the right pictures in the right order, you can command attention for a long time.

TAKEAWAY: *Lead with the eye and the mind will follow. The longer you give your audience something interesting to look at, the longer they will give you their mind.*

CHAPTER 5

START WITH THE *WHO*

I'm curious about other people. That's the essence of my acting. I'm interested in what it would be like to be you.
—MERYL STREEP

Picture Order Matters Because People Matter

The six pictures you just saw are guaranteed to help clarify your own thinking. That's because they're a direct reflection of the way your visual mind looks at the world. If you want to solve a problem, draw out the pieces in order. By the time you've drawn number 3 (your **map**) or number 4 (your **timeline**), you'll begin to see a possible solution to your problem, and you'll see your idea with renewed clarity.

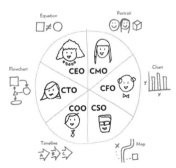

But what about showing your pictures to other people? What about making a presentation, or providing guidance, or selling an idea, or teaching someone—does the order of the pictures matter then? Absolutely. It matters because you are a *person*, and so is everyone else.

People Love People

Great minds discuss ideas; average minds discuss events; small minds discuss people.

—ELEANOR ROOSEVELT

Eleanor Roosevelt was a genius, but this time she got it wrong. It's not only small-minded people who talk about other people; *everybody* talks about other people. And we all talk about other people all the time; even when you do talk about ideas or events, 90 percent of the time you're talking about the people involved. It's human nature: People love to know what other people are up to. My first job after college was as a graphic designer at a San Francisco weekly newspaper. We were going through a redesign and our art director, John, had a vision. Since people love to talk about other people, we decided to try a new design and editorial direction. We still told the same news, but we made people the center of the news stories.

We stopped putting elaborate political cartoons on the cover of the newspaper and started putting nicely photographed portraits of the newsmakers' faces instead. For the first time in years, circulation soared.

I learned a lesson that has stayed with me ever since. People do care about ideas, and people do care about events, but more than anything else, *people care about people*.

People Are at the Heart of Everything

There were so many websites on the Internet . . . but there was no service to help us find the most important thing to our lives: people.

—MARK ZUCKERBERG

No matter what your job is, at the heart of your work you're always going to find people. To win in what you do, you will need to see those people, know something about them, and recognize their individual qualities. You will need to draw distinctions between them. And yes, sometimes you will need to draw them.

If we look deeply into most problems, we will find people.

But if we look deeply into people, we will find our solutions.

Show the *Who* First

You can make more friends in two months by becoming genuinely interested in other people than you can in two years by trying to get other people interested in you.

—DALE CARNEGIE

If you want to engage your audience's mind, show them people. If you want to engage their heart, show them themselves.

When you want to get people involved in your idea, the first thing you should show them is *who is involved*. Not just who is at fault, or who is the victim, or who is the winner, but everybody. When you see a football game on TV, the first thing broadcast is a lineup of the players. When you go to a play, the first thing they hand you is the playbill, which tells you all the characters you're about to meet. When you attend a project kickoff meeting, the first thing that should happen is for everyone to introduce themselves.

It's not just good policy to identify the people first; as far as your visual mind is concerned, it's the law. The reason your visual What Pathway identifies people first is because without players there's no game.

But all people aren't equal. As far as your mind is concerned, one player almost always takes precedence over all others: *you*. And that's true for everybody.

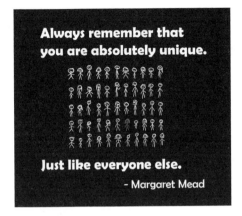

So if you want to engage your audience's heart, first show them where they fit into your idea. When people see where your idea impacts them, they will pay rapt attention to the what, where, when, how, and why.

Q: What's the best way to show *who*?
A: Faces.

Of all the visual capacity you have in your brain, an enormous amount is dedicated to faces: seeing them, remembering them, and recognizing them. To prove how extraordinary your facial recognition skills are, here's a little thought exercise.

It's impossible to imagine how many different faces you have seen in your lifetime, so let's start small. Imagine walking down a city street. How many people's faces to do see? A few dozen, at least. Now stop at a newsstand and leaf through a magazine. How many faces do you see on the pages? Maybe fifty? Now take your seat in a movie theater and look around before the show. How many faces do you see? A couple hundred, at least. Now rush through the airport: another five hundred faces. Now walk down Fifth Avenue: a thousand more. And that's just one day.

Now multiply that by the number of busy days you have in a year. No matter where you live, within a few short years, you're likely to see millions of different faces. *Millions of faces*—and all with two eyes, a nose, and a mouth.

Now think about how many times to you have really, truly mistaken one person for another. It's not very often; you can probably count those events—*OMG, I really thought you were my friend Jane!*—on one hand. The fact that you make this kind of mistake so rarely in relation to the total number of people you see daily proves how powerful your visual memory is. Now, that's a lot of fine-tuned mental capacity you *want* to access when you communicate. That's why you show *people*.

You See Faces in Everything

More than anything else, it really does come down to faces. We look at clouds, we see faces. We look at electrical plugs, we see faces. We look at burnt toast, we see faces. In 1994, Diana Duyser, a homemaker in Florida, saw the Virgin Mary's face in her grilled cheese sandwich and saved the sandwich in a sealed box. And she wasn't alone; when Diana put the sandwich up for auction on eBay ten years later, an online gambling site bought it for $28,000.

You look at cars and you really see faces. Car makers know this and use your visual mind to try to sell you their cars. The *Wall Street Journal* put it like this: "Car makers have long talked about the 'face' of a car—headlights for eyes, grille for a mouth and the bumper as jaws—and auto designers say the difference between a hit and a flop may come down to a vehicle's visage."

This explains why if you think cars are getting meaner looking, you're right. Marketing studies done by the auto manufacturers show that in our world of increasingly aggressive traffic, we prefer to drive cars that look scarier. *Welcome to my freeway; now get out of my way.*

Hello.   Eat me.

It's a subconscious buying decision driven by a phenomenon called "pareidolia": your visual mind's unstoppable attempt to see patterns shared between things that aren't anything alike. In other words, you see faces in everything.

And why wouldn't you? With so much energy invested in facial recognition, it's only natural your brain would use that capacity all the time—even for things that aren't faces. A recent study published in the *Proceedings of the National Academy of Sciences* had auto experts look at the fronts of cars, and the same area of the brain involved in facial recognition was activated.

Same area in the brain!

The takeaway? Use people and faces to generate interest in what you want to share. If you can make something look like a face, you're guaranteed that people will see it.

Welcome to Whoville

There are five simple pictorial ways to add people to your presentations, reports, and lessons.

1. Just draw a circle and give it a person's name. Fast and amazingly effective for giving visual character to a name.
2. Draw an emoticon—a smiley face, a frowny face; with a little practice, you can convey almost any emotion immediately.
3. Sketch a stick figure. (My favorite—and more on this in a minute.)
4. Draw a slightly more detailed "block" figure. A little harder to draw, but great to show action.

5. Quickly sketch a "star" figure. Superfast and supereffective, especially if you need to draw a lot of people fast.

The Right Way to Draw a Stick Figure

People aren't shaped the way you think they are. Back when you were a little kid with a crayon, drawing stick figures in preschool, you drew people's heads a lot bigger than they actually are. That was simply a reflection of how your brain saw things, driven by your innate powers of perception.

As a tiny baby, the very first thing your brain told your eyes to look for was a face. And not just any face, but the face of your *mother*. When you were helpless and completely dependent on someone else to take care of you, you had eyes only for her. Hopefully, when you looked up, you saw Mom, and her protective face took up your whole field of vision.

No wonder we all think people's faces are large; we like people with big heads. And we still do.

Q: Why did you hire Vanna (White)?
A: Because she had a big head.

Many of the great Hollywood stars—Joan Crawford, Bette Davis, even Marilyn Monroe—had outsize heads. For some reason the camera compensates for the disparity by making their features stand out, thus causing them to appear more attractive on-screen.

—MERV GRIFFIN

Head size as a proportion of body height:

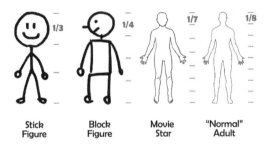

| Stick Figure | Block Figure | Movie Star | "Normal" Adult |

When you draw a stick figure, don't even try to make the proportions accurate. After analyzing thousands of stick figures, comparing those that look "right" with those that look weird, it seems to me that the ideal proportions follow the *rule of thirds*:

Head = ⅓ total height
Body = ⅓ total height
Legs = ⅓ total height

If you draw a simple stick figure according to this formula, your audience will see the figure and think, "That's a normal-looking person" and focus on what the figure *represents*. If not—if your figure's head is too small or legs too long—your audience will see a badly drawn stick figure, note that something is off, and focus on trying to figure out what is wrong about your drawing.

So, grab a pen and follow along with me as we draw the ideal stick figure:

1. Start with the head by drawing a circle. (Remember Chapter 3!)
2. Draw a single line down, equal in length to the head.
3. Add two legs, each the same length as the body.
4. Draw two arms, again, the same length as the legs. (And don't forget to leave a neck!)
5. Add two eyes and a mouth. (*Never* add a nose; they're impossible to draw and just distract.)
6. Finally, add little circles for the hands and feet. Presto: perfect figure.

Once you know this formula, and with a little practice, you will find that you can create dozens of different figures doing hundreds of things. All you need to do is shift the angles of the body and limbs, and when you're feeling really adventurous, bend the arms and legs a bit.

Anthropomorphize Everything

"Anthropomorphize" is a fancy word that summarizes everything in this chapter: If you want people to take notice and pay attention to things, make those things look like people. This works in two ways: the *give-it-a-face* approach and the *make-it-human-sized* approach.

1. Give your idea a face by including people at the heart of your explanation.

The next time you need to explain a concept, don't talk about a faceless black box. Black boxes sound sexy, but in the end they all look alike and don't attract attention for long. Instead, create a quick map of the people involved.

TAX PAYERS = TAX PLAYERS

I was recently asked by a big accounting firm to help shake up their tax department. Their people were awesome at calculating, reporting, and filing taxes on behalf of their clients, but in the quickly changing regulatory world of global organizations and shifting accounting standards, that's less than half the battle. In this new world, tax planning and strategy are the real differentiators. But their people struggled to sell that service. Not because they didn't see the goal, but because they'd never drawn it. So that's what we did—and we put people at the center.

First, we drew a set of simple portraits, illustrating all the main players in the corporate tax world: executives, regulators, investors, and of course the tax department.

CORPORATE TAX PLAYERS

Then we simply asked, "What do all these people do all day?" To answer that, we created a map of "Tax," showing the core elements and processes, supported by technologies and measures.

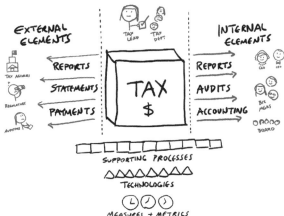

Now, the tax teams and clients can literally see where they fit—and the sales process visually speaks for itself.

2. Make data come to life by showing it on a human scale.

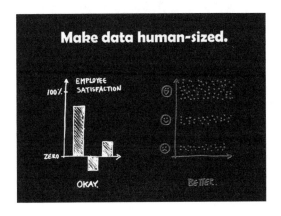

Bar charts are cold. "This is strictly business," they say. "Nothing personal or human here; *these are not the insights you're looking for.*" What a lie. Data is alive, and when abstracted into boxes, it quickly loses its meaning. It might be fine to depersonalize data when you need to say, "It's nothing personal; it's just business," but it seems to me that good business is *always* personal.

Even worse, when everything is presented in a bar chart, everything looks the same—and before long no one remembers what they're looking at. Money, time, people, attention, and growth—the things most frequently accounted for in charts—are all wildly different concepts, each interesting in its own right, and all fascinating when put together. To help people dive into this fascination, show the data on a human scale.

HOW OLD ARE PICTURES?

In preparing for this book, I was researching how long people have been drawing; 32,000 years is the latest answer, based on the carbon dating of the organic pigments found in the ancient Chauvet Cave in southern France. "Thirty-two thousand years," I said to myself. "That seems like a long time." But how long is it? The only way to know a number that big is to see it. So I decided to make a chart. But my chart doesn't show years; it shows *people*.

For the purpose of my own visual understanding, I decided to assume that a single human generation—from one parent to one child—lasts 25 years. (Averaged over the history of humanity, it's probably closer to 15 to 20 years, but the math is easier and the result is pretty similar either way.)

So if you draw a little stick figure to represent each generation . . .

$$\text{↟} = 1 \text{ generation} = 25 \text{ yrs}$$

You can then draw a chart showing every single generation going back to the beginning of recorded history roughly 5,000 years ago.

History is short.

BEGINNING OF RECORDED HISTORY
(INVENTION OF WRITING - MIDDLE EAST)

That's it; only 200 generations of humans have existed since the ancient Egyptians started writing stuff down (with drawings, of course). When I saw this, my mind was blown. I had always thought history was long. Now I see the truth; it isn't.

When you give data, ideas, and concepts a human face, you bring them to life—and then everybody wants to look.

Chapter Checklist

❑ More than anything else, people are interested in other people.

❑ Learning to add simple emoticons and stick figures to charts and diagrams helps you bring your data to life.

❑ When you add human elements to your ideas, you radically increase your audience's attention and their desire to know more.

TAKEAWAY: *If you want to capture attention, show people.*

CHAPTER 6

TO LEAD, DRAW YOUR DESTINATION

In order to carry a positive action we must develop here a positive vision.

—DALAI LAMA

Why Comes After *Who*

First you drew the *who*. That got their attention. But people won't follow you for long if they can't see where you're going. So if you want to lead others, you need to draw your goal, the big *why* at the end of the journey.

To effectively draw your goal you need to first have a pretty clear idea of where you want to go. Second, you need to find a visual way to communicate that destination. That's why your next picture will be a vision.

TWO VISIONS THAT STILL SHINE TODAY

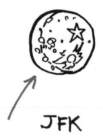

JFK

In the greatest presidential vision statement of all time, John F. Kennedy gave America a crystal clear destination. He simply looked up. "We choose to go to the moon," he said. "We choose to go to the moon this decade and do the other things, not because they are easy, but because they are hard." In this simple statement Kennedy clearly mapped out his vision for us, the American people. Our destination? The moon. Our journey? The challenge of doing everything necessary to get there. Our *why*? Succeed or fail, we will be a better people for the effort.

MLK

When Martin Luther King Jr. called out his vision for America with "I have a dream," he began by reminding the quarter-million listeners gathered in Washington of a promise made to American slaves one hundred years before. Citing Lincoln's Emancipation Proclamation, he said, "It came as a joyous daybreak to end the long night of their captivity." Then he reminded the country that although the night still wasn't over, he had a dream of the coming daybreak. Our destination? A new morning in America. Our journey? We will walk toward it together. Our *why*? To prevail.

Of the thousands of speeches delivered by thousands of politicians and thinkers in the fifty years since, why are these two particular speeches so often remembered and quoted? Because both are grand visions made *visible*. Whether the goal is landing on the moon or "that day when all of God's children . . . will be able to join hands and sing," the destinations can literally be seen. And for leaders and followers, this vision matters.

A recent study highlighted in the *Harvard Business Review* revealed that US presidents who used image-based words in their speeches were considered to be more charismatic than those who didn't. "These findings suggest that the successful articulation and enactment of a leader's vision may rest on his or her ability to *paint followers a verbal picture* of what can be accomplished with their help" (emphasis mine).

Now imagine if you painted that picture . . . with a picture.

Vision Statements Are a Lie

At some point every leader is tasked with creating a vision statement, a short verbal description of an organization's mission, purpose, and values. That's great, but wait: Shouldn't a *vision* statement include a picture? After all, vision statements aren't called "Wordy jargon statements that nobody believes, remembers, or cares about." But that's how most end up. Think about it. When was the last time you read an organization's vision statement that motivated you to put down whatever you were doing and follow it?

Vision statements fail for two primary reasons: First, they don't typically contain a destination that can be reached or a goal that can be won, and second, by trying to account for everything an organization stands for, they usually end up saying nothing.

A vision statement should be a statement of a destination and purpose, of course, but it must also function as a short story (a *very* short story) that captivates the audience's whole being: ears, eyes, mind, and heart. There is a simple way to do this, and two thousand years ago Aristotle already had it figured out: For a story to capture someone's interest, it must have a hero, the hero must have a conflict, and that conflict must be a *singular*. If your hero is trying to fix six things, it's hard to keep rooting for her.

Leader, You Are on a Quest

From my grandfather to my father, this has come to me. They dreamt of the day when the Dwarves of Erebor would reclaim their homeland. There is no choice, Balin. Not for me.

—THORIN OAKENSHIELD, *THE HOBBIT: AN UNEXPECTED JOURNEY*

As a leader, you are on a quest. You are taking your team to a specific goal, and among the thousand things that job demands, none is more important than your ability to describe that destination. If you're the coach of a basketball team, your destination is winning the game—or at least losing with honor. If you're the service-company CEO, your destination is profitable customer satisfaction.

If you're the chief trial lawyer, your destination is a verdict resoundingly in your client's favor. If you're the technology team leader, your destination is delivering the best possible solution—on time and on budget.

Every leader has such a quest—often several of them, one following the next. To succeed at each step, you must see your destination and then show it to your team. This isn't a walk around the block; this is your vision quest.

A goal is not always meant to be reached; it often serves simply as something to aim at.

—BRUCE LEE

Every Quest Starts with a Hero

At the center of every quest is a hero, the person (or group) seeking to improve life—either for himself or herself, or for the benefit of someone else. As a leader, that hero could be you, it could be your team, it could be your brand, it could be your company, or best of all, it could be your customer.

Hero

At the heart of every quest is the desire for someone to become happier, more successful, or more complete. When you know whose life you are hoping to make better, you've identified your hero.

The Seven Classic Quests

There is a reason that *Star Wars*, *The Lord of the Rings*, *Harry Potter*, and Marvel's *Avengers* are the most popular movies of all time—and from any quantitative measure, the most successful entertainment franchises in history. Their creators know many things about character development, setting, and plot—but they also never forget three critical rules about storytelling: First, everyone loves to be part of a quest; second, the canon of great quests is small; and three, the first two rules have been true since the beginning of time.

No matter what your business, organization, or team does to operate on a day-to-day basis, it's likely that your true vision—your true destination—falls into one of seven classic quests. Find that quest, and you've found your vision.

What is your quest?

1. Trying to get back home
2. Striving to win the prize
3. Seeking to exact revenge for a previous humiliation
4. Fighting to slay the dragon
5. Working to be reborn as a better person
6. Laboring to climb the mountain
7. Searching for true love

These quests are at the core of the classic story archetypes, and serve over and over as the basis of the tales we tell ourselves. Obviously, they are all metaphors—there are no real dragons on earth to be slayed, there are not many mountains left to climb, and true love increasingly seems impossible to find—but that doesn't stop the most ancient parts of your brain from trying.

7 Classic Quests

As leader, your task is to find the classic quest that most closely guides your purpose, use that to guide the creation of your true vision statement, and from that, create the symbol that points the way.

Your vision will become clear only when you can look into your own heart. Who looks outside, dreams; who looks inside, awakes.

—CARL JUNG

Your Job? Create Your Mission Patch.

Think of teams that share a goal: a football team on its way to the Super Bowl, the astronauts on the first mission to Mars, the marines storming the beach, the Girl Scouts selling you Thin Mints. Beyond a single objective and a leader to guide them there, what else do they have in common? They all have a mission patch.

Make your mission patch.

Your mission patch is your destination made visible. It is a simple picture that, when glanced at—even for a heartbeat—reminds you of where you hope to go. It serves as a nonverbal map of direction and destination, an icon that expresses your idea, belief, or brand perfectly without saying a word. A mission patch is a visual good luck charm to keep in your pocket and look at if you lose your way. It is your talisman, an instant reminder of home.

Home

A SYMBOL IS AN INSTANT REMINDER OF HOME.

According to *Fortune* magazine, the following are the symbols of the world's top dozen brands this year. Forget vision statements,

CEO speeches, and annual reports; what do these *mission patches* mean to you? Look at them for a moment and feel your reaction. It's right there, isn't it? You know what these symbols mean without easily being able to *say* what they mean. That's what you're looking for. That's *vision*. Now let's find you yours.

Clarity Is Key

Clarity is the most important thing. I can compare clarity to pruning in gardening . . . If you are not clear, nothing is going to happen.

—DIANE VON FURSTENBERG

To create your team's mission patch, you will need two things: first, clarity of destination, and second, a picture to express it. Clarity usually comes from one of two paths: finding your true passion or determining your business objective. If you are truly blessed, they might both be the same.

Because there are countless ways to find your own vision, setting up guide rails helps point you along your path. In my work of helping leaders find their path, I like to present the tale of Jack and Diane, two American business leaders who rose to prominence during the years I started paying attention to communications:

longtime ABC News commentator Diane Sawyer and longtime GE CEO Jack Welch.

Jack and Diane were both wildly successful in their careers and, according to most measures, equally successful in their lives. Yet Jack and Diane represent near polar opposites in the way they talk about their successes. Diane says, "Passion first, then business." Jack says, "Business first, then passion." There is a lot you can learn about your path from comparing these two.

TABLE OF VISION CLARITY		
Visionary leader	Diane Sawyer	Jack Welch
Path to clarity	PASSION FIRST, THEN BUSINESS	BUSINESS FIRST, THEN PASSION
Quote	"Follow what you are genuinely passionate about and let that guide you to your destination."	"Good business leaders create a vision, articulate the vision, passionately own the vision, and relentlessly drive it to completion."

Mission patch		
Driving motive	Love your life and your work will follow.	Love your work and your life will follow.
Approach	Pay attention to what you are good at and enjoy. Do that well, and your path will become clear.	Pay attention to what your business, competitors, and customers are doing well—or poorly. Fixing the bad and being better at the good will shape your path. Then be relentless.
Leadership	When people see your genuine passion for what you do, they will line up to join you on your quest.	When people see that you are crystal clear on what guides your success, they will line up to follow you.

Either Way Works, but Remember That It's Your Quest

Let these two paths inspire you as you look for your own clarity—but remember, although your quest will look like many others, the path you lead will be your own.

Now to Find Your Picture . . .

To find your vision picture, look back to the seven quests as your starting point. These classics are rich with meaning, history, inspiration, and examples you can dive into as you discover your visual destination.

Get home. Your journey home is your return to the promised land, the most classic of quests. Whether taking back your mountain (*The Hobbit*), sailing home from war (the *Odyssey*), or battling endless obstacles to reach your loved ones (*The Martian*), all people understand the power of getting back home.

This is Motel 6 saying, "We'll leave the light on for you."

Your "get home" leadership vision might be:

- Retake your rightful market share (Steve Jobs returning to Apple).
- Help your customers reunite with their families (Red Cross).

Win the prize. As a classic quest, "win the prize" takes on different forms, such as winning the race (*Seabiscuit, Around the World in 80 Days*) or beating the obstacles to discover your better, stronger self (*Rocky, Charlie and the Chocolate Factory*). No matter the prize or the obstacles in the end, the real race is against yourself.

This is Nike saying, "Just do it."

Your "win the prize" leadership vision might be:

- Offer the best customer service in the world (Zappos).
- Beat every competitor in every field you choose to operate in (GE).

Get revenge. It might not be pretty, but exacting revenge on the ones who wronged you has an undeniable sweetness (*The Count of*

Monte Cristo). Righteous indignation has driven as many quests as anything in our better nature (*Hamlet*, the Crusades). This is the darkest of quest motives, but make no mistake: Revenge really motivates.

This is Carrie Underwood taking a key to his pretty little four-wheel drive.

Your "get revenge" leadership vision might be:

- Take down the team that took you down (Yankees and Red Sox).
- Finally beat the competition (Chevy Silverado and Ford F-150).
- Improve by trying to catch the competition (Pepsi and Coca-Cola).

Slay the dragon. Long before Beowulf went after the monster Grendel 1,500 years ago, slaying the dragon had been at the heart of more quests than anything else. Whether a real dragon (*The Hobbit*, again), or the Death Star (*Star Wars*), or the devil within (*A Beautiful Mind*), nothing motivates better than killing the beast that is bent on killing you.

This is Avon pulling out all the stops to stop cancer.

Your "slay the dragon" leadership vision might be:

- Destroy educational limitations (Khan Academy).
- Kill software (Salesforce).

Be reborn. This is the deepest and most personal of all quests because being reborn means losing the fight so that your spirit comes back stronger (Obi-Wan Kenobi in *Star Wars*). This is the ultimate "Hero's Journey," sacrificing your comfortable life through suffering so that you will become a better version of yourself (*Avatar*).

This is Howard Schultz shutting down every Starbucks in America in 2008 for a global reset.

Your "being reborn" leadership vision might be:

- Close down for forty-seven years, waiting for the right moment to return (*Vanity Fair* magazine).
- Scale back all operations in order to retool and rethink—and come back with a vengeance (LEGO).

Climb the mountain. Winning the gold is one thing; people watch and cheer. Scaling the peak is another—no medals, deathly cold, and lonely; it's just you, the mountain, and the elements. This is any trek in which the end is uncertain, but you do it anyway (*All Is Lost, 127 Hours*). If you undertake this quest for fame, you will lose (*Into Thin Air*). This is a task you undertake not for monetary gain, but because it is there—and you will be a better person for the effort.

This is Marvel Comics keeping at the same stories for fifty long years—finally to become the most successful film studio in decades.

Your "climb the mountain" leadership vision might be:

- Make incremental improvements in a business that nobody thought would ever succeed (Western Union turning down Alexander Graham Bell's telephone concept).
- Keep at your "dumb" dream until everyone finally sees how great it is (Ben & Jerry's).

Find true love. The last great quest is that of your heart; finding true love in a world of deception, cynicism, and anger (*Romeo and Juliet, Twilight*). Just when it seems that matches made in heaven have to go through hell, you find your other half, and suddenly become complete (*50 First Dates*—or any rom-com ever filmed). Even if you have to give it up, the quest was always worth the pain (*Casablanca*).

This is Disney buying Pixar, a business match made in Hollywood heaven.

Your "find true love" leadership vision might be:

- Offer a product for the simple reason that you love it so much (Burton Snowboards).
- Help your hero customers find each other (Tinder).

Mix and Match

This little library of quests covers so much ground because these tales come from our deepest needs as people: shelter, food, security, and companionship—all made more desirable by the lure of adventure. With a clear purpose and a visible destination, you are ready to lead.

To Manage, Draw the Map

Anytime I feel lost, I pull out a map and stare. I stare until I have reminded myself that life is a giant adventure, so much to do, to see.

—ANGELINA JOLIE

Mission patch ready, your destination is clear and your *visual* vision is ready to share. When your team sees so clearly where you are leading them, their first comment will be, "Let's go." Then they will look to you, and their first question will be in the form of, "Um . . . so how do we get there?" And that's when you draw the map.

Don't confuse your destination with the process you'll take to get there; that's a different picture altogether. Your mission patch showed the destination—but you'll need a map to show the steps.

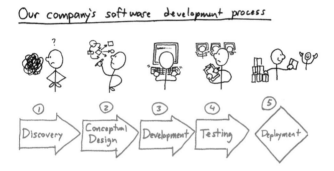

Our company's software development process

1. Discovery
2. Conceptual Design
3. Development
4. Testing
5. Deployment

Mapping your process steps could be a book in itself. (In fact, it is: *Business Process Management* books are plentiful.) But what matters for us are two things. First, you need to know that mapping is a visual process. If you want people to see the steps you want them to take, you'll need to draw them a picture of those steps.

As a visual process, drawing your map is an excellent way to make sure you have a process and show that you know it. First, draw a starting arrow to show where you are now. Then—far away on the right—draw your destination. Then, with a series of connected arrows, fill in the steps between. There may be few steps or there may be many—and if you have multiple people and projects, there will likely be multiple parallel paths—but either way, if you find a gap, you'll know what you need to improve.

The second point to remember is that making a map isn't leadership; it's management. You'll need a map to show how to get where you're going, but as the leader, you'll first need to show why.

Map out your future—but do it in pencil.

—JON BON JOVI

Chapter Checklist

- ☐ As a leader, your number one job is to provide vision—and that requires a picture.

- ☐ When people can see what you are asking them to do, they are infinitely more willing (and able) to do it.

- ☐ The core library of vision archetypes is small; learn it, and you can inspire extraordinary action with few images.

- ☐ Once your destination is clear, you'll make the "management map" that shows how to get there.

TAKEAWAY: *If you want to people to follow, first show your destination.*

CHAPTER 7

TO SELL, DRAW TOGETHER

Maybe you don't hold the title of salesperson, but if the business you are in requires you to deal with people, you, my friend, are in sales.

—ZIG ZIGLAR

The Sales Journey

Finding your true leadership vision is most likely a journey you will take on your own. Selling is different; sales is always a journey you share with someone else. Why does this matter to you? Because no matter what your business goal or your personal vision is, you're going to need to sell it.

Sales Is Big

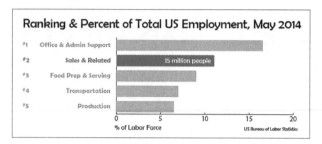

Ranking & Percent of Total US Employment, May 2014

#		
#1	Office & Admin Support	
#2	Sales & Related	15 million people
#3	Food Prep & Serving	
#4	Transportation	
#5	Production	

% of Labor Force

US Bureau of Labor Statistics

According to the US Bureau of Labor Statistics, "sales" is the second largest profession in the United States, employing fifteen million people. But if we're realistic about what sales means, it involves a lot more people than that—everybody, in fact.

Yes, sales is the well-dressed guy fitting your shoes, the broker on the phone, the tech consultant showing you the latest cool hardware, and the smiling face at the cosmetics counter. But sales is also you trying to get your kid to eat broccoli, your partner convincing you to cut down on the red wine and go hit the gym, and your colleague going to the boss for a raise.

Sales is broad to describe but simple to define: Anytime you're trying to get someone to take a new action, you're selling. Getting yourself off your chair requires a decision, discipline, and habit. Getting someone else off their chair requires sales.

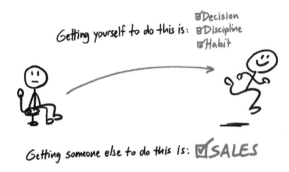

Your Secret Weapon

The difference between you and the person not reading this book is that you are about to have a secret weapon: visual sales. Which makes you a kind of sales Jedi.

Most people who sell professionally have been taught any number of sales techniques, negotiation styles, deal-making principles, and consultative approaches. That's great, and in the right hands those work well. But what those people have not been taught is the most basic and powerful sales tool of all: drawing pictures.

Talk the Way People Think

If you're trying to persuade people to do something, or buy something, it seems to me you should use their language, the language they use every day, the language in which they think.

—**DAVID OGILVY**

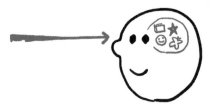

Although you don't think about it much, most people think more in pictures than through words—or anything else. (Remember our brain data from Chapter 4.) So if you want to use the most common human language, use pictures. Visual sales simply means engaging the eyes of your prospect and using that as an entry point to seize her visual mind.

This approach works. Partly that's because visual sales is unusual, partly because it is unexpected, and partly because it is fun—which in sales is particularly refreshing. But the real reason visual sales works is because by activating your prospect's visual mind, you are giving her exactly what her brain wants most: a clear picture of your idea, stripped of as many words as possible.

When I worked at a small brand and strategy consulting company in New York, every single time we used this visual sales approach in a pitch, we won. Every time we planned, researched, and drew a new way of looking at the prospect's problem, we won the sale—even when we weren't the biggest or most experienced competitor. We won major projects at big companies, leading scientific organizations, and even other consultancies, often surprising ourselves.

We called this approach "finding the million-dollar chart," and with a little practice, it isn't that hard. Whether your sales target is one million dollars or one thousand or one hundred or just getting someone moving, this approach will work for you.

Pictures Sell Products

It's been known forever that pictures sell products. You see Jennifer Aniston drinking a bottle of Smartwater and you want to drink Smartwater. You see a Ferrari and you want a Ferrari. You see the dude rocking with his white Apple earbuds and you want that

Apple iPod. Or maybe you *want* Jen or the dude, or to *be* Jen or the dude—either way, that's the point. You see something appealing and you want it.

Pictures clearly work to sell a product. But what about using pictures to sell an idea? That's where visual sales comes in. It is a thinking approach that helps you create the right picture to sell an idea—and then appear magical as you draw that idea right in front of your prospect. (You won't actually be drawing most of it at all, but we'll get to that in a minute.)

The Mind-Meld, Part 1

By drawing your idea with your prospect—by literally starting the drawing and then handing over the pen—you create a mind-meld that can't be generated any other way. In other words, *you draw your prospect in by drawing your thoughts out.*

Your picture is a shared vision that you create together. But just because you're sharing the pen does not mean that your roles are equal. You're the actor and your prospect is the audience. You are playing a well-researched and well-prepared part. You've rehearsed that part well enough so that your confidence in your drawing reassures your audience and gives her the confidence to join in.

Basically, you're selling a world as an actor, right? I mean it's like any sales person: if you believe in your product, you know your product, you sell it a lot better.

—PAUL WALKER

But just because you're an actor, it doesn't mean you're faking anything. On the contrary, the power of visual sales is that it's almost impossible *not* to be authentic. Because your lines—both spoken and drawn—are real and rehearsed, they reflect what you believe in. So you will not only look genuine to your audience; you will be genuine. (An added benefit is that you will also appear spontaneous and almost magically smart.)

So What Picture Should You Draw?

You've already got a quiver full of pictures: simple stick figures, elaborate circles, basic maps, sequential timelines, and cause-and-effect flowcharts. Depending on what you're selling—and to whom you are selling it—any one of these might be your best visual sales starting point. But before you get to that decision, there is one more aspect of visual selling you need to know; and this one concept will become your visual sales friend and fallback.

Q: What's the oldest advertising play in the world?
A: Before and after.

If selling is you trying to get someone to take action, the very best way to make your case is to simply show what things look like now, before the action, and then show what things will look like later, after the action is done. It is your easiest, most direct, and most reliable way to motivate because if you and your prospect can see the result, you are both infinitely more likely to believe it is possible.

Before & After

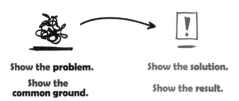

Show the problem.   Show the solution.

Show the common ground.   Show the result.

The classic before-and-after method works brilliantly for visual sales. First, you create a simple picture that summarizes the problem and the *common ground* you share with your prospect. Then you change the picture to show the result; what things will look like when the problem is solved. Sure, the win isn't guaranteed, but one thing is absolutely certain: If you can't see what the *after* state might look like, you will never get there. By drawing the goal state for all of your visual sales pitches, you give yourself and your prospect the target to aim for.

DRAW THE CHANGE YOU DESIRE;
BASIC BEFORE-AND-AFTER VISUAL TEMPLATES

The visual change	The *before* problems you're solving; the *after* solutions you're proposing

Bend the line.

Before: The line is trending down. Sales are off from last year. Customers are leaving.

After: Let's bend the line back up. Let's recover those sales. Let's get those customers back—plus a bunch of new ones!

Hit this number.

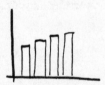   

Before: Sales are up, but they could be better. Maybe we're missing a potential part of the market. Maybe our expectations could be higher.

After: Let's reset projections higher. Let's get more aggressive with our goals. Let's let the motor rip and see how high we can go.

The visual change	The *before* problems you're solving; the *after* solutions you're proposing

Link these pieces.

Before: Things are a mess. We've got pieces all over the place and don't know how they fit together. Nothing is working well.

After: Let's see what it looks like when all the pieces are in the right place. Let's sketch out how the operation will function when it's a well-oiled machine.

Eliminate these steps.

Before: This is the way things have always been done. This is our standard operating procedure. This is why it takes so long to do stuff.

After: Let's see if we can't cut out or bypass a couple of these steps. If we reorder the sequence, maybe we speed things up and reduce redundancy.

continued . . .

The visual change	The *before* problems you're solving; the *after* solutions you're proposing
Focus on this.	
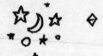	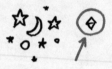
Before: We're so busy and distracted, we don't know what is most important—or how to prioritize. What should we be looking at?	After: Let's take a look at this outlier; it might be nothing—or it could be the most important piece we're neglecting.

These simple *before-and-afters* almost always work as the basic backbone for visual sales. And they're not difficult to create. Look back at the drawings in the table above. Recognize them? They're the same **charts**, **maps**, and **timelines** you drew way back in Chapter 3.

Yes, these simple pictures are the same elemental drawings triggered by your visual system: a *before-and-after chart* for sales involving quantities and numbers, a *before-and-after map* for sales involving the position and interaction of things, and a *before-and-after timeline* for sales involving sequences of events.

Build Your Library

Not all sales are the same; selling a chief information officer an enterprise-wide cybersecurity system is different from convincing your spouse to go skiing on the coldest weekend of the year, which is different from getting you to choose my favorite hot sauce next time you're in the supermarket. But pictures will help in every case. So you'll want to develop a go-to library of picture types you can rely on for different sales challenges.

1. Sales about results

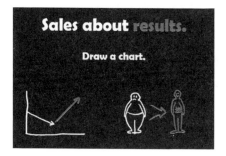

When you're selling numbers to results-oriented people, you will draw a before-and-after chart. Your first drawing shows the present numbers and trends, and your second drawing shows that upward bend in the line and the desired result.

When you're selling to salespeople, finance pros, fitness junkies, bookkeepers, or harried doctors, before-and-after charts are the best way to sell ideas that drive more sales, ensure faster ROI, guarantee quicker calorie burn, reduce tax payments, or deliver better clinical outcomes.

2. Sales about solutions

When you are selling a solution to someone facing a problem with many moving pieces, you will draw a before-and-after map or flowchart. Your first drawing shows the various pieces laid out in the present-day arrangement, emphasizing missing connections or even disarray. Your second drawing shows all the pieces coming together in order, creating a clearly improved state of affairs.

When you're selling to strategy-oriented executives, technical architects and process engineers, small-business owners, or overwhelmed new parents, before-and-after maps are the best way to sell ideas that make priorities clearer, systems that run more smoothly, software that makes complex things simpler to do, and secrets that make life a little less frantic.

3. Sales about desire

When you are selling desire, you will draw the vision. Remember Jennifer Aniston's Smartwater, the Ferrari, and the dude jamming out to his music? Those are all simple visions of what people want: beauty, clarity, movement, speed, joy, and happiness. This drawing is the only one that doesn't need a *before*; just drawing the *after* is enough. People will get the message.

When you're selling the perfect way to blow a few thousand bucks to a just-minted millionaire, a dream wedding to an excited bride, or a road trip to the high-school junior who just passed the driving test, drawing the vision of what's possible is the greatest sales picture ever. When you're selling the dream, you just need to remind the mind's eye what it looks like.

The Mind-Meld, Part 2: 75–25

All of these sales journeys are at least a two-person task—you and your prospect—so to make the drawing process complete, you will need to share the pen. That's easy because you're an actor now, and a well-rehearsed one. How well rehearsed? Seventy-five percent.

The ideal visual sale involves you drawing 75 percent of your chart, map, timeline, or vision, then handing over the pen and helping your prospect draw the remaining 25 percent. And at that point, the drawing is no longer yours; it's your prospect's.

This handoff is the real beginning of the sale. You got the drawing started and, because you were rehearsed and confident, your prospect saw where you were going, and wove your picture into her thinking. With your pen in her hand, she will show you exactly what she wants.

You don't just have a sale going now; you have a real conversation taking place. And all because you drew.

To Do That, You've Got to Plan

To make this work, you've got to do your homework in advance. Learn as much as you can about who you'll be handing the pen to, learn even more about the problem she needs to solve, and learn everything about the idea you want to sell to solve it.

To prepare 75 percent of your drawing in advance you have two options: Option A, you create your drawing (by hand, via software, or by hiring a designer), scan it, and then print it out. Bring the printout to your meeting, show it to your prospect as you explain what it illustrates—marking up highlights as you talk—and then hand over the pen. Ask your prospect to circle what's most important to her, scratch out whatever is incorrect, or add anything missing. If you're genuine in your interest, it's almost inevitable that your prospect will start marking up the drawing as well.

Option B is exactly the same, except for one thing: Instead of printing out your 75 percent drawing, commit it to memory and practice drawing it a few times while narrating your thoughts. Then when you sit down with your prospect, draw the picture from memory, explaining as you go. This is pure magic, and forms a sales bond unlike anything else.

**Option A: Bring a printout
and mark it up.**

**Option B: Bring a blank
and draw it live.**

The Proof Is in the Planning

Three years ago, the CEO of London's iconic Burberry fashion house
flew to San Francisco on a vision quest. Having run Burberry for
six years, Angela Ahrendts had successfully transformed the company from a purveyor of beige trench coats and plaid scarves to a
reenergized fashion powerhouse. Now she needed a new technology platform to support her vision of the company as a constant
fashion companion to her growing customer base.

According to *Fortune* magazine, Angela had heard that Marc
Benioff, CEO of the cloud-computing giant Salesforce, was the
man to meet. In tech circles, he was known for having visions even
bigger than her own. When they met, Marc listened to Angela's
ideas, then pulled out a napkin and started drawing.

Starting with a stick figure to represent the Burberry customer,
he added circles to show platforms like Facebook and Twitter,
channels like mobile and stores, systems like SAP, and interactions
like games and interactive content. Marc talked as he drew, paus-
ing to listen to questions and ideas from Angela, then adding new
circles as he went, linking everything together in a single grand
vision of people, technology, and content.

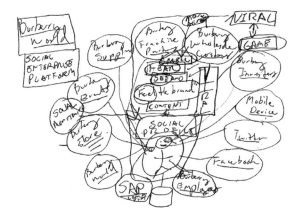

After twenty minutes, Marc added a title: "Burberry World Social Enterprise Platform." Angela was impressed. Not only had Marc listened to her, he had created this entire universe in minutes. Of course she hired Salesforce to build the platform Marc drew; given the way he drew it, that was a foregone conclusion. But even more important, she saw unfold before her eyes the power of technology to enable retail sales in ways she hadn't thought of before.

A year later, and partly inspired by Marc's drawing, Angela left Burberry to become the new head of retail at Apple—and the most highly paid executive at the company.

It's the greatest story of visual sales in years. And the most important part? While it might have looked to Angela like Marc was creating his amazing picture on the spot, in fact he had been rehearsing it for months with his teams at Salesforce. This is the power of 75–25.

Perception Is Reality; Perception Comes from Picture

In sales, it's not what you say; it's how they perceive what you say.

—JEFFREY GITOMER

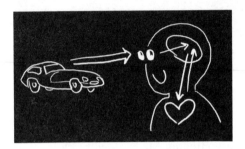

Pictures are the fastest way to your prospect's heart. If you're looking to enhance their perception, draw them in.

Chapter Checklist

☐ Sales is the art of getting someone to take a new action; a picture creates the ideal mind-meld.

☐ Learn to draw your prospect in by drawing your thoughts out.

☐ To make sales magic, use the 75–25 rule: Draw 75 percent of your picture in advance and 25 percent during your pitch.

TAKEAWAY: *If you want to sell, you have to take the visual journey together.*

CHAPTER 8

TO INNOVATE, DRAW THE WORLD UPSIDE DOWN

Business has only two functions—marketing and innovation.

—MILAN KUNDERA

The Endless Gold Rush

As I write this, I am in San Francisco, the American city universally recognized for sustained technological innovation. That so much reinvention has taken place here makes sense. San Francisco is, after all, a city whose entire history can be told through a tale of gold rushes. Some succeeded, some failed, and from day one, the DNA of San Francisco was defined by a cycle of rises, falls, and renewals, or in other words, innovation.

Innovation Is Gold

If you think of it in terms of the Gold Rush, you'd be pretty depressed right now because the last nugget of gold would be gone. But the good thing is, with innovation, there isn't a last nugget. Every new thing creates two new questions and two new opportunities.

—JEFF BEZOS

"Innovation" is the most sustained business buzzword of the last decade. "We're going to innovate our way out of this slump," says the embattled tech executive to Wall Street. "We're going to become the Apple/Uber/Airbnb of _____ industry," says the entrepreneur seeking venture capital dollars. "Innovation distinguishes between a leader and a follower," said Steve Jobs, from the center of it all.

But what innovation actually means—and why it's necessary at all—still isn't that clear. Which is probably why most of us really aren't that good at it. But if you start with a circle and give it a name, you will be.

Why Innovate?

BECAUSE ...

$$\square + \triangle = \bigcirc$$

You might remember this visual equation from Chapter 3. It simply reminds you why innovation is important: because no matter how good you are at doing what you do now, our rapidly changing world is sooner or later going to demand that you do something else.

This chapter will show you how to use the visual tools you've already learned to do exactly that: how to look at old things with a fresh pair of eyes.

When Is a Good Time to Innovate?

The simple answer for when you should use the set of visual innovation prompts described in this chapter is . . . well, always. Innovation isn't something you should do once in a while; innovation is like breathing: It's got an in-phase and an out-phase, and if you stop doing it for long, you die.

There will be times when someone says to you, "Let's think outside the box." That would be a good time to turn to this chapter and say right back, "Okay, and I know exactly how to do that." Then again, there will be times when someone says to you, "Just shut up and do it." That would be an even better time to turn to this chapter and say, "Fine, but let me see if I can find a better way to get it done."

What Is Innovation?

The best definition I've seen of innovation comes (and I don't think this will surprise you) in the shape of a circle. On the right side, the circle curves into an arrow called "pattern breaking." On the left side, the arrow circles back around as "pattern optimizing."

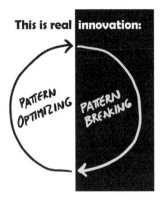

Pattern breaking is the kind of innovation that makes headlines, and is exactly what it sounds like. Somebody—Jeff Bezos or Mark Zuckerberg or Angela Ahrendts—looks at an existing industry and sees a way to completely transform it, often creating an entirely new way of doing things along the way.

Pattern breaking is also Amazon turning the retail world on its head and leaving monster retailers in ruins, Uber changing overnight the way millions of people think about getting to work, and Salman Khan of the Khan Academy inspiring tenured Stanford University professors to quit their day jobs and start online universities. (If you remember drawing your business break-lines back in Chapter 1, you were probably drawing a pattern-breaking competitor.)

On the left side of the circle is pattern optimization, a less glamorous (yet frequently more effective) style of innovation. Pattern optimization is Toyota refining every nuance of auto manufacturing so finely that no competitor can keep up with their relentless pace of tiny improvements. It is a now-dominant Amazon adding Amazon Prime to further capture the wallet-share of dedicated online buyers or your local flower shop increasing sales by building an email list of shopper birthdays.

The beauty of this simple circle is that it illustrates the never-ending nature of true innovation. When you try something crazy-new and it fails, you start over—but if it works, it becomes the "new normal." Then you optimize the heck out of it, squeezing every drop of efficiency you can . . . until someone else comes along and pattern breaks you right out of existence.

The Real Trick to Innovation

An innovation, to grow organically from within, has to be based on an intact tradition.

—YO-YO MA

What many people who want to be innovators forget is that to pattern break or pattern optimize, there first has to be a pattern.

Take roller skates. In the mid 1980s an entirely new type of skate appeared almost overnight, called the in-line, and it transformed the industry. Before, roller skates were seen mainly indoors and in the dark: roller rinks, roller derbies, and roller boogies. Now, millions of people who had never skated in the light of day discovered a fabulous new exercise, and Rollerblades became a household name.

"INNOVATION" ALWAYS HAS A PAST:

1905

1920-1980

1980 —

Although Rollerblades seemed completely new, they were really just a simple twist on the clunky two-by-two-wheel truck design that had existed almost unchanged for sixty years, which were themselves a simple twist on the original roller skates—which look almost identical to today's in-line skates.

This shows that the fastest and simplest way to become an innovator is to get good at looking at things as they are, and then turning that idea upside down—and that's where your drawing comes in.

Visual Innovation Prompts

Visual innovation prompts are quick, proven ways to use simple pictures to generate new ideas from old ones. The process is not hard. First, you need to find or create some kind of simple picture illustrating what a standard thing, process, or idea looks like today. (This could be a portrait, a timeline, a map, and so on.)

Capturing this "as-is" picture does two things for your innovation engine. First, it ensures that you have thought through the original problem and recognize that there is an accepted, status quo solution. This is your starting point. Second, you apply one of the visual innovation prompts to your picture and see what kind of results you get.

In the case of your roller skates, one innovation prompt you could make use of is "break up and recombine."

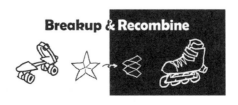

Start with four wide wheels in two side-by-side tracks and a place to put your foot. Cut up the pieces and rearrange them. Presto: the creation of inline skates.

Five Essential Visual Innovation Prompts

I'm going to show you five more such prompts. They are a good and powerful starting point for you to immediately become a great visual innovator. Once you understand the basic thinking behind each of them, I guarantee you will discover dozens more.

1. Flip it backward.

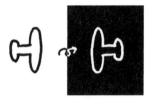

The first airplane had half of its tail on the front. It was wildly unstable and almost impossible to fly. The Wright brothers, who started out building bicycles, liked it that way. They sold a few "Wright Flyers" and made a little money. Their archcompetitor, Glenn Curtiss, built his first airplane the same way, but suspected that he would sell a lot more if he made his airplanes more stable, so he drew his next design with the tail at the back.

It worked. By the end of the first decade of flight, the Wrights were bankrupt and Curtiss owned the largest airplane company on earth. His approach defined aircraft design for more than sixty years.

But innovation always cycles. In the 1970s, a designer named Burt Rutan came along and drew his entire airplane backward—tail at the front, engine and wings at the back—and discovered that his airplane literally could not stall in the air. Rutan kept designing backward airplanes until his team won the $10 million Ansari X Prize for the first successful private spaceship. Then Burt retired.

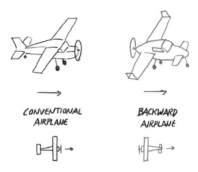

CONVENTIONAL
AIRPLANE

BACKWARD
AIRPLANE

The same "backward" prompt brought about the most radical shift ever in software design: Agile. In the early days of software design, you first collected every conceivable requirement, nailed down everything in a "waterfall" project plan, then started to code. Months, sometimes years, later you deployed. But it took so long to get it done that by the time you finished, the requirements had usually changed.

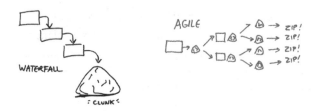

By the 1970s, some innovative developers realized that if they reversed this process they got better and faster results. So they gathered a single requirement, quickly built a piece of code to do just that, tested it, and then made fixes as they started the next cycle. It took a while to catch on, but now you'd be hard-pressed to find any developer who doesn't use the "backward" Agile approach to software design.

2. Turn it upside down.

A few years ago a multilevel marketing company asked me to help with their communications. I had no idea what an MLM was, so I looked it up. "Oh," said the Internet, "that's a pyramid scheme." I politely told the company, "No."

But they pursued me, asked me to test their products (which were good), and explained how their sales model actually worked in the real world.

I found this company's approach intriguing, and—for the appropriately hungry and ethically solid salesperson—a powerful way to get a good product into customers' hands without the typically massive advertising and marketing spend. Legal and innovative; it sounded like fun to me.

"Yes," I said, "but the first thing we've got to do is redraw your sales model." Why? Because every time they explained to me how their sales worked, they always drew a pyramid. Which always made it look like a scam.

One late afternoon, after a long session of whiteboarding sales models, I was driving home on autopilot mode, admiring the beautiful oak trees along the freeway, when it hit me. "Turn the pyramid upside down! Make it a tree!"

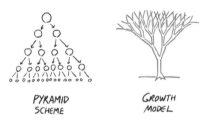

PYRAMID
SCHEME

GROWTH
MODEL

Everyone hates a pyramid scheme; even if it is ethical and legal, it always looks like the people on the bottom are squashed. Who would want to join that? But everyone loves a tree. Who wouldn't want to be the top leaf on the top branch, growing upward into the light? Communication problem solved.

3. Oppose it.

What happens when you take something you know works and intentionally do the exact opposite? Disaster, usually. But not always. If you really want to find a new way to win, you might be surprised what happens when you make white into black, day into night, or tech tools into toys.

My team was as surprised as anyone when we unexpectedly won a project with the consulting giant McKinsey & Company—by selling them the exact opposite of what they asked us to do. This is a risky approach, but if you're selling innovation, it sometimes works.

McKinsey had issued a request for proposal (RFP) to several vendors for an innovative technology project. They were very specific about how the written proposals and in-person presentations needed to be structured.

Given our team's inexperience pitching to McKinsey, we figured there was no chance we would win. So we filled out the paperwork as proscribed, including all requested technical details and project plans and measurable outcomes, but decided we had nothing to lose by discarding the instructions for the live presentation.

Before the meeting, we built a model of our concept using LEGO bricks. Substituting LEGOs for data elements helped us visualize the end state of the project and reverse engineer (at a conceptual level) how we might build it. We took photos of the LEGO model in various phases of construction and structured our presentation around those pictures.

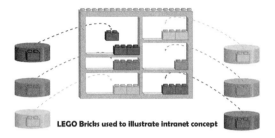

LEGO Bricks used to illustrate intranet concept

The McKinsey team were so surprised when we showed them LEGOS that, after a moment of initial shock, they invited us stay longer than our allocated time. And we won the project.

From the perspective of the McKinsey team, our presentation was an example of what is known as a "black swan" event. Since every presentation they had ever seen followed a predicable flow (as demanded by their own RFPs), it never occurred to them that they'd see anything else. And when they did, they saw real innovation, and—thankfully in this case—appreciated it for the real problem-solving that it was.

4. Put it in a box.

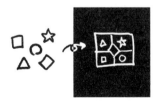

Over the past six years, one of the bestselling books on business strategy, *Business Model Generation*, proved to be an innovation in and of itself: Not only was it originally self-published, but according to traditional business schools, it isn't even a strategy book.

Created by Alexander Osterwalder and Yves Pigneur working in concert with two-hundred-plus contributors, *Business Model Generation* defined an entirely new way of looking at business planning and started a worldwide revolution in how business models are created, used, and perceived.

The centerpiece of the book is the Business Model Canvas, a deceptively simple game board containing nine separate zones. There is nothing new about what is in each zone: business activities, customers, costs, key resources, channels—these are essential business concepts that have been taught for decades.

What is new and innovative (and frankly brilliant) is that Alex and Yves found a way to force-fit all the pieces together into a common frame, and in doing so revealed *in a visual way* the underlying connections between them all—many of which had never before been seen so clearly.

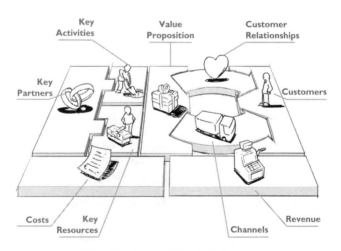

The Business Model Canvas

Like many breakthrough frameworks, from the periodic table of the elements to the rotating-ring structure of DNA to the US Constitution, once you look at the Business Model Canvas, your immediate response is, "Of course it's like that. How else could it be?"

It is an example of the creative freedom of constraint (more on this in a minute), illustrating the fact that when you intentionally set out to put everything in a box, you invariably see new and unexpected connections appear.

Yes, you might damage something, but that's exactly why it's called "pattern breaking."

5. Reduce the number of pieces.

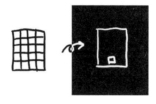

On January 9, 2007, Steve Jobs introduced the iPhone. As with all Apple product launches, it was a great stage show, with Steve in classic-casual form, magic stage props, etc.—you know the drill. If you go back now and watch the keynote, you will see many moments of carefully crafted stage drama.

But the transition that stands out to me as the critical moment, the true "OMG, you did it again!" comes at the 0:05:07 mark. After haranguing the not-very-smart capabilities of "smart" phones, Steve pops up a photo of the four leading models. And of course they are covered with buttons; how else would they function?

Then he shows us how. It's called the iPhone, and it has one button. Sold.

Yes, there is a lot more than that, and the ten thousand songs and the photos and the visual voice mail are nice, but . . . well, in the words of Steve quoting an Apple engineer, "You had me at scroll."

The next time you need to find a new way to do something, build something, serve something, or sell something, try the "reduce the number of pieces" prompt; what would it look like and how would it work if it only had one button?

Embrace the Freedom of Constraint

The enemy of art is the absence of limitations.

—ORSON WELLES

As an innovator, limitations really are your best friend. If everything is possible, picking any one path is impossible. Luckily, you're a visual innovator, so setting helpful limits is easy:

- Use unlimited sheets of paper as you think, but no more than seven when you present.
- Use the whole whiteboard, but stop the meeting when it's full.
- Use no more than three colors.
- Think increasingly big for half the time, then think increasingly small.
- Start with vision; end with planning.

Give Your Innovation Some Time

Remember, the automobile, the airplane, the telephone, these were all considered toys at their introduction because they had no constituency. They were too new.

—NOLAN BUSHNELL

Vincent van Gogh is both the least successful and most successful artist of all time. He didn't sell a single painting in his lifetime, yet his paintings now sell at the highest prices ever paid for art. As you start to draw more for your life and your business, I wouldn't necessarily set that as your mission, but there is inspiration for innovation there still.

Plan to Succeed, but Prepare to Fail

There is no innovation and creativity without failure. Period.

—BRENÉ BROWN

Sometimes your idea will be better than the original; sometimes it will be worse. But the most important rule that experienced innovators know is this: Failure *is always* an option.

If you don't try something, nothing will happen.

I disagree with those in the innovation field who say that you should plan to fail. Unless you've got the endless cash flow of Google, that's not a sustainable model. You should plan to *succeed*—but recognize that some failure along the way is inevitable. And that's a good thing.

Visual innovation prompts	Visual trick
1. Flip it backward. 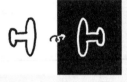	Move the beginning to the end. Rearrange the order. Flip the direction. Examples: Agile programming: Code first, then collect requirements. Jet engines: Give them away for free but charge for maintenance. Canard airplane: Move the tail to the front to make it safer and faster.
2. Turn it upside down. 	Flip it over. Move the base to the top. Turn a stable mountain into a wobbling teeter-totter. Examples: A pyramid scheme becomes a tree of growth. A sales funnel becomes a mug with the cream on top. A wineglass becomes a bug trap.
3. Oppose it. 	Look for the opposite. Turn white to black. Turn a question into an answer. Expect the unexpected. Examples: Short a hot market. Sell when everyone else is buying. Garden at night. Sail west to reach the Orient.

4. Put it in a box.

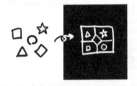

Put pieces together that don't want to go together. Force-fit things into a too-small container. Find a single model that accounts for everything.

Examples: Reese's Peanut Butter Cups. Swiss Army knife. The Business Model Canvas.

5. Reduce the number of pieces.

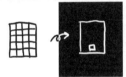

Take out everything that isn't absolutely critical. Combine many functions into one. Get rid of buttons. Travel light.

Examples: The iPhone. All-in-one printer/scanner/fax. Draw with just two colors out of the sixty-four-color box. Pack one bag for your ascent on Everest.

Chapter Checklist

- ❏ Innovation simply means, "Learning to look at old things in new ways."
- ❏ The best way look at something with new eyes is to turn it upside down (or any of four other visual innovation prompts).
- ❏ Because we get used to things as they are, we easily become blind to the obvious. Refreshing our point of view fixes that.

TAKEAWAY: *If you want to create something new, first draw something old. Then turn it upside down.*

CHAPTER 9

TO TRAIN, DRAW THE STORY

I have come to believe that a great teacher is a great artist and that there are as few as there are any other great artists.

—JOHN STEINBECK

The Ultimate Business Skill

Something they don't teach you in business school is how much of business involves teaching. As a project manager, you've got to teach your team to read your project plan. As an IT lead, you've got to teach the staff how to keep their online identities safe. As an accountant, you've got to teach non-finance people how to make sense of their time sheets. As a lawyer, you've got to train everyone how to *not* get the business sued. Conservatively speaking, I'd say that half of sales requires teaching, most of strategy is teaching, and almost all of consulting is teaching.

You might remember this drawing, from way back in Chapter 2, showing the four essential aspects of winning in business. We've covered the first three: leadership, sales, and innovation; how could you succeed without those? But it's the fourth aspect of winning in business that often gets forgotten—and that's a mistake.

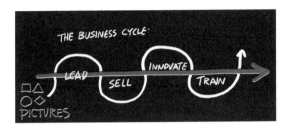

No business works without workers, no business thrives without new blood, and no business continuity is possible without people who already know how things work. *Training* is frequently neglected in businesses and invariably becomes the first target of cost cutting when times get tough, even though in the long run effective teaching is your most important profit center. But only if your teaching is good.

Those Who Can't Do

The best CEOs I know are teachers, and at the core of what they teach is strategy.

—MICHAEL PORTER

There is an old axiom from George Bernard Shaw: "He who can, does. He who cannot, teaches." The phrase has stuck around ever since and is usually used to justify why teachers get paid so little. But it's wrong.

The real axiom ought to be a circle that reads, *"Those who can't do, teach. Those who can't teach, consult. And those who can't consult, have to get back to work.*" In other words, it's a loop, and we're all caught up in it—just as we should be.

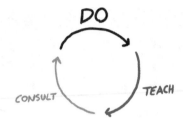

In the professional world, if you're doing your job right, you should spin around this circle at least a couple of times a year. First, you spend a bunch of time getting your work done. (That's the *doing.*) Then you have to explain to somebody else what you've done. (That's *teaching.*) Then, if you've explained it well (or especially if you didn't), you will be asked to document why you did it that way. (That's *consulting.*) Then the cycle repeats.

Why does this matter? Because at some point, no matter what you do, you will need to be the teacher.

Flying with Dad

I like a teacher who gives you something to take home to think about besides homework.

—LILY TOMLIN

My dad had two careers, executive training and flying. For his day job, he taught government employees how to work more effectively as teams, and on weekends he taught people to fly. For his executive presentations, I remember helping Dad sort endless piles of

35 mm slides into carousels, building visual stories picture by picture. (My job today is similar, only now I use PowerPoint instead of Kodak.)

I also spent hundreds of hours sitting next to him in the cockpit of a small plane. As a teaching environment, an airplane cockpit is pretty awful: It's noisy, bouncy, smelly, sweltering (or freezing), often boring—and then suddenly terrifying. But with a good teacher, learning to fly is enthralling and life changing. Happily, I had a good teacher, and from my dad I learned many good lessons on how to train people.

For example, when teaching a complex task, break it down into steps. Make sure one step is clear before going on to the next.

Another lesson is the *talk-do-talk-do* process: First explain to the student what you're going to do, then do it. Then explain it again, and have the student do it. Then ask the student to explain what they just did. Then have them do it again. It's a great way for your student to rapidly gain competence and confidence.

The third lesson is the most effective for your student—and for you, as teacher, the most difficult: After you've completed the steps above, give your pen (or in my dad's case, the plane) to your student, and let them finish the lesson on their own.

Teach It Forward

Experience is the teacher of all things.

—**JULIUS CAESAR**

Taking the time to teach someone what you do is often the hardest part of your job. If you're anything like me, you're too busy *doing* to take the time to train someone else to do it. But I also know that every time you do take the time, it always helps later, because then there is someone already prepared to help when your big break comes along—or when you just need to take a break.

Here's a training secret that took me a long time to realize: Since the human brain is hardwired to want to learn, teaching is easier than most people think. All you really need to do is make your process clear, provide an achievable target and well-defined directions—and then get out of the way.

This might initially feel a little weird, but it's a good teaching trick: The more opportunity you give your students to do the work for themselves (in other words, the less you *preach*), the more your students will love your teaching.

No matter where you sit in your organization, this chapter will help you be a better teacher by becoming a *visual* teacher. That means two things: First, you will see how to create a simple six-picture visual story to explain anything, and second, you will see when it is time to be quiet and turn over the pen.

Story Time

Now that you've been with me for a while in this book, I very much hope for two things: I hope that you like the pictures we've drawn so far, and I hope that thinking about them has helped you discover something new about your purpose, your values, and your own creativity.

But you're not quite done yet. Although you've created good pictures to help you lead, sell, and innovate, you can't assume that you have a good visual story that you can *teach*. You have the pieces, but they're not yet a story; they will only become a story when you weave them all together into a visual narrative with a beginning, middle, and end.

A good visual story is one that tells the *whole* story. The story begins with a quick scene introducing *who* or *what* you're talking about. Scene two then assigns measurable *quantities* to those people or things. The next scene maps the relative *positions* of your players and elements, the following scene lines up the *sequence* in which they interact, the next scene illustrates the *cause-and-effect* relationships that emerge between them, and the final scene concludes with the big *aha* takeaway lesson.

If you want to see something interesting, go back through that paragraph above and count how many scenes it includes. If you come up with six (and if I did the math right, you should), a little bell might go off in your head: *Six . . . you've seen that number before: It's the number of pictures your visual mind sees when understanding the world.*

You can be confident that the story above is good for teaching an idea for one simple reason: because it is derived directly from the six steps of how your students see.

Show Your Story in Six Pictures

To create the ideal teachable story, use all of the six elemental pictures *in sequence* to build a complete visual narrative. Done right—which is easy if you follow the steps of vision—your visual story will provide all the context your audience needs to follow along, and the insight they need to take over later.

The ideal visual story contains these six pictures, presented in this order:

1. **Who and what are involved.** Open every teaching story with a visual summary of the people and things you are going to be talking about.

2. **How many are involved.** Next, provide a quantitative measure (or many measures) of the people or things. Changes in number (trends) are particularly revealing.

3. **Where the pieces are located.** Present a map illustrating the relative positions of these people or things according to geographical or conceptual coordinates.

4. **When things occur.** Next, show a timeline that illustrates the sequence in which these people or things interact, or the steps required to bring them into alignment.

5. **How things impact each other.** Provide a flowchart that adds cause-and-effect influences superimposed on any (or all) of your previous pictures; show the change and how you will achieve it.

6. **Why this matters.** Complete your visual story with a concluding visual equation that summarizes the keep learnings, takeaways, or action items triggered by the previous visual insights.

These six pictures are summarized in this illustration:

The Ideal Six-Picture Storyline:

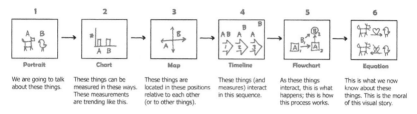

1	2	3	4	5	6
Portrait	Chart	Map	Timeline	Flowchart	Equation
We are going to talk about these things.	These things can be measured in these ways. These measurements are trending like this.	These things are located in these positions relative to each other (or to other things).	These things (and measures) interact in this sequence.	As these things interact, this is what happens; this is how this process works.	This is what we now know about these things. This is the moral of this visual story.

The ideal visual story is built as a series of six increasingly elaborate pictures that mirror the process of vision. Told this way, any idea—no matter how complex—can be clarified by harnessing the power of the visual cognition system.

How to Get a Raise . . .

Here's an example. Your friend has been working at a firm for a little over a year. He has done a great job and enjoys his work, and believes it is time for a raise. Knowing that you've successfully negotiated your own raises in the past, he asks for advice. You know from your own experience that asking for a raise is a tricky and stressful action, so you create this little visual story to guide your friend.

The story you tell	The picture you draw	The words you say
An important business lesson in six pictures: ## How to get a raise.	You're just talking, so no picture yet . . .	*There are good ways and bad ways to ask for a raise. Here is an approach that I've learned works well.*
The scenario: ## You need a raise. **To get that raise, you're going to give a presentation to your boss.** You are going to convince her that you can contribute so much more to the firm that she is going to <u>want</u> to pay you more.	. . . not yet . . .	*In asking for a raise, you're going to give a mini-presentation to your boss. You are going to convince her that you can contribute so much more to the firm that she is going to want to pay you more.*

The story you tell	The picture you draw	The words you say
Picture 1A: Who is involved? <u>**You, your boss, and the firm are the players.**</u> 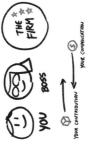 **Picture 1B:** What is involved? <u>**Your contribution and your compensation are the goal.**</u>	Picture 1 is a **portrait** showing the people and things involved in getting a raise.	*There are three "people" involved in getting a raise, and two "things." The people are you, your boss, and the firm. The things are your contribution to the firm and your compensation from the firm.*
Picture 2: How much is involved? <u>**You will contribute this much more to the firm.**</u> 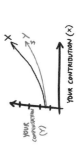 **In acknowledgment, the firm should <u>increase</u> your compensation by <u>this much</u>.**	Picture 2 is a **chart** illustrating a measurable aspect of elements from Picture 1.	*You're going to set a measurable quantity to your new contribution to the firm—selling more items, taking on more responsibility, etc.—which will be met by a measurable increase in your compensation.*

The story you tell	The picture you draw	The words you say
Picture 3: Where are the pieces — before and after? **Today, you, your boss, and the firm overlap, but you will increase that overlap by becoming a greater contributor to the key activities of the company.** 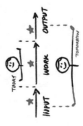	Picture 3 is a before-and-after map showing the overlap of the pieces and things you identified in Picture 1.	*Today, you're involved in the firm and its key activities, but you'd like to be more deeply committed and more directly contribute to those activities.*
Picture 4A: What is the sequence now? **Today, work comes in, you do it, and then you hand it off.** Picture 4B: What will be the new sequence? **Tomorrow, you will actively seek out key work, do it, and then guide it to completion.** 	Picture 4 is a before-and-after timeline showing the order in which elements occur.	*Today, work basically comes to you, you do it, and then you hand it off. What you'd like to do is actively seek out the work, continue to do it well, and then be more involved in driving it to completion.*

The story you tell	The picture you draw	The words you say

The story you tell

Picture 5: How will this take place?
You will dedicate yourself to improving these key activities of the firm. Your success will be measured according to this metric.

In exchange, your compensation should increase by this amount.

Picture 6: Why is this a good idea for all the players?
This is a good long-term idea because your contribution will improve the firm more than it costs the firm.

The picture you draw

Picture 5 is a **flowchart** illustrating how you're going to rearrange the elements for a better outcome.

Picture 6 is an **equation** showing the improved end state.

The words you say

To make this happen, you will dedicate yourself to improving specific key activities of the firm so that your improvement can be measured. In exchange, you would like your compensation to increase by an equally specific amount.

In the end, this is a better deal for you and the firm, as you strongly believe that your renewed commitment will earn the firm more than it costs.

That's how the six-picture explanation works. By presenting all the pieces in sequential pictures in order of increasing complexity, you can teach any idea.

Feel Free to Riff a Bit

Not all visual stories require all six pictures to become clear, and sometimes you may find that your story becomes more compelling by switching the order a bit. Experiment as you build your visual sequence, but keep these rules in mind:

- Every explanation should begin with the portrait illustrating who and what are the key players. (See Chapter 5 for a refresher on starting with *who*.)
- Every explanation should include a *why*—either up front or as the conclusion. This is either your mission patch purpose or the visual moral of the story. (See Chapter 6 for a refresher on *vision*.)
- Every explanation should include some kind of measurable attribute, element, or trend. This makes even the highest-minded concept reconnect with reality, and helps your students know that you're not blowing smoke.
- Remember where these six pictures come from: They are drawn directly from the process of vision. If you choose to leave any out, make sure you have a good reason for doing so; you could well be leaving out the one picture that your students most need to see.

Hand over the Pen

We discovered that education is not something which the teacher does, but that it is a natural process which develops spontaneously in the human being.

—MARIA MONTESSORI

Once you've shared the story, it's time to hand over the pen so that your student can complete the work himself or herself.

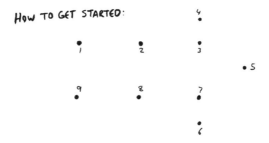

In the lesson in the visual story above, you taught your friend a thoughtful way to go about getting a raise. That's a good thing—but your friend isn't yet ready to go ask. Why? Because he hasn't himself done any work. You showed him that he was going to have to draw six pictures for his boss, but those specific pictures—the chart, the map, the timeline, etc.—are still undrawn.

So now you're going to help your friend a second time, this time by helping him connect those dots himself. Luckily for both of you, the best "hand over the pen" exercise is just that: You create the dots and then he connects them.

For example, you could draw this and hand it over:

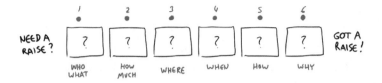

When you think about training as connecting the dots, the process becomes simple and self-sustaining: First, you map out the big picture of your idea, then identify the inflection points (where critical decisions are made, where problems crop up or breakthroughs take place) and put a dot next to each one. Then stop, hand over the pen, and say, "Here; you finish."

For example, here's one more picture to help your friend. Whether he gets his raise or not, the most critical lesson is that getting a raise is about making a deal—and a deal is always a two-way street. So you could draw one last picture to help him really understand that message.

This time, you draw a summary of the players and the result—but leave the connecting lines off:

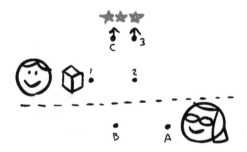

Then ask him to connect the dots:

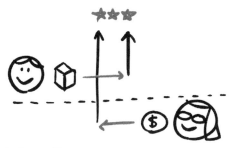

And that's the real lesson.

Picture 6b) The lesson:

A raise is a <u>two-way</u> street.

Find a way to <u>show</u> your boss that you know that, and it will be easy for her to say <u>Yes.</u>
(Or at least hard to say no.)

Flying with a Whiteboard

The truth is that anything significant that happens in math, science, or engineering is the result of heightened intuition and creativity. This is art by another name, and it's something that tests are not very good at identifying or measuring.

—SALMAN KHAN

Things really do come full circle. After I gave my dad a copy of my first book, *The Back of the Napkin*, he added a new step to his flight-training regime: an in-flight whiteboard. When words fail, when there are too many, or when lengthy conversation is challenging (like in the cockpit of a small plane), draw out the lesson in real time. This captivates the student, clarifies the confusing, gives everyone's brain a chance to take a break—and makes lessons stick.

Chapter Checklist

❑ If you're too busy to train someone else to do what you do, you're too busy to really succeed.

❑ Teach anything by drawing it out in six sequential pictures.

❑ The best training is connecting the dots; when you hand over the pen, you both learn more.

TAKEAWAY: *Training isn't a time drain; training is a knowledge gain.*

CHAPTER 10

WHEN IN DOUBT, DRAW IT OUT

Open your eyes and look within.

—BOB MARLEY

What Your Eyes Help You Do

Your eyes do one thing: They make sense of the visible world. They do it constantly, they do it continuously, and they do it without any conscious effort on your part. Vision is your superpower. It would be a waste not to use your vision as well as you can, and a sin not to improve it.

You already own all the tools you need; the hardware was there from your birth, and the software booted up the moment you first opened your eyes. Now all you need to do is keep upgrading. That's what this book is really about, and I hope these lessons have helped.

Before we wrap up, there is one more picture story I want to share.

The Million-Word Picture

I drew pictures of the characters. Nobody's ever seen these before either. These were just things I did for my own.

—J. K. ROWLING

At over 450 million copies sold, the seven books of *Harry Potter* run 4,224 pages in length, contain 1,084,170 words, and together compose the bestselling book series in history. What few people know is that in order to organize her thinking for this monumental undertaking, J. K. Rowling drew frequently during her writing process. She drew her characters, her settings, and elaborate time-lines to keep track of who was doing what and when.

For anyone working through the complex puzzle that is success, this is an important lesson: Simple drawings clarify complexity. But J. K. Rowling's belief in pictures goes even further than that—and offers another useful lesson: A thoughtful picture can support a million words.

In the seventh and final *Harry Potter* book, J. K. Rowling introduces a single, simple symbol that serves to visually summarize the entire series. Containing a circle, a triangle, and a line, the "Deathly Hallows" weaves together and unifies the three most important concepts in the books: love, protection, and magic. As the reader, this mission patch guides you through to the last page.

Wouldn't it be incredible if you could offer your business audiences the same thing? How valuable would it be for you to have a simple picture that you could quickly draw when you need to summarize a complex concept, remember all the pieces of your project, or convey your entire strategy?

I ask this because, as we near the end of this book, I'd like to offer you similar visual guidance.

The ABCs of Drawing

Imagine visual thinking in its most elemental form; think about what drawings and pictures and images mean to you and your success, at their most basic level.

AWARENESS

A = Awareness. *Drawing enhances your awareness.* More than any of your other senses, vision makes you aware of the world around you. You see people and you know who you are engaged with. You see collections and quantities and you know how many things you have at your disposal. You see the positions of things and know how they might fit together, and where you might fit in. In the words of Harry Houdini, "What the eyes see and the ears hear, the mind believes."

B = Beauty. *Drawing makes ideas beautiful.* There's no denying it; lines are elegant and light is beautiful. Your eyes simply love to look at things. Yes, there are terrifying images out there and many things you'd rather not see, but colors are always amazing, shapes evocative, and visual puzzles compelling, and your eyes relish trying to figure things out. Although your drawings might not be gorgeous, creating them always adds a little beauty to the business of the day.

C = Clarity. *Drawing makes things clear.* The goal of drawing ideas isn't to make them simplistic; it is to make them clear. Trying to force complexity through the funnel of language is a wonderful thinking exercise but often masks hidden connections and ignores nonlinear relationships. Forcing underlying patterns to the surface by drawing them out makes previously invisible solutions become visible.

C = **Comprehension**. *Drawing makes things understandable*. Your visual mind has a lot of horsepower behind it; it is really good at making sense of things even when facing an overwhelming amount of incoming information. Equally important, when you see something wrong, you know it's wrong—even if you can't verbally describe why. If you can find or create the pictures that describe your thinking, you can be pretty sure that other people will be able to see the same things.

C = **Communication**. *Drawing makes things shareable*. Pictures are the fastest way to get ideas into the brain. When you see something simple and clear, your brain thinks it is interesting long before you consciously know you're even looking at it. That's the final reason to use pictures: because as useful as drawing is to you to help find answers, it's even more effective at getting other people to see exactly what you mean.

This Book's Mission Patch

Put together those ABCs into a picture and you get the final mission patch for this book: the star of awareness surrounded by the circle of beauty, all enclosed within the arrows of clarity, comprehension, and communication.

THE POWER OF VISION

The next time someone asks you why you draw in meetings, go ahead and draw them that. As you draw, tell them, "Pictures increase awareness, add a little beauty to business, and improve clarity, comprehension, and communication." I think they'll get it.

Your Visual Mind Is Smart

I couldn't beat people with my strength; I don't have a hard shot; I'm not the quickest skater in the league. My eyes and my mind have to do most of the work.

—WAYNE GRETZKY

The next time you're not sure what is going on at work, or you're struggling to define the best market position for your product, or you're wondering how to fix a snarled-up process problem, or you simply can't remember why you're doing what you're doing, do yourself a favor. Pick up a pen and a piece of paper, and draw a circle. Name that circle the first thing that comes to mind. Then draw a second circle, and ask, "What should I call this one?" Then keep going.

Wax on, wax off. Lather, rinse, repeat. Fake it until you make it. By the time you've drawn six circles, you'll begin to see your answer.

Don't give up until you see something you hadn't thought of before. It will happen; your visual mind guarantees it.

My Last Word on Pictures

Vision is your friend. Vision is your guide. Vision is your protector. Learn to use it. No matter what success challenge lies before you—leadership, sales, innovation, training, or other—you will find your best solutions by using your whole brain. Simply put, that means *don't forget your pictures.*

When in doubt, draw it out.

Chapter Checklist

❑ The right picture can support a million words.

❑ Pictures increase your awareness, add a little beauty to business, and improve clarity, comprehension, and communication.

❑ When you understand your visual mind, you give yourself a magnificent gift: the power to really see.

TAKEAWAY: *When something is unclear, start drawing. It will unleash the problem-solving power of your visual mind.*

ACKNOWLEDGMENTS

A book is one big idea and fifty thousand words flying in tight formation. It takes a lot of hands to keep those words (and pictures) pointing in the right direction, and I'd like to thank everyone who lent me theirs.

First, thanks to Adrian Zackheim, Will Weisser, and Jesse Maeshiro at Portfolio/Penguin, who encouraged me to pull together in one place the best of everything I have to share. Thank you Ted Weinstein, my agent of ten years, for insisting that I could do it, and keeping me focused throughout.

Thank you Tom Neilssen, Les Tuerk, Michele DiLisio, Marge Hennessey, and the whole crew at the BrightSight Group for getting me in front of tens of thousands of people so that I could share, test, and refine these ideas in real time.

Speaking of real time, I wrote this book chapter by chapter with the help, guidance, and patient participation of nearly 250 of my NapkinAcademy.com associates. For the ten months it took to write this book, they stayed with me every step of the way, giving me continual feedback on everything from the title to the structure to the individual drawings. If I hadn't had the opportunity to share the book with them throughout the process, I'm pretty sure I never would have managed to finish it. So special thanks to: Anderson Willis, Stacy Davis, Keith Campbell, Gordon Sato, Ronald Palagi, Christine Krimmel, Dwayne Clark, Patricio Romeo, Dimas Edwards, Nikki Myles, Derrick Kuhn, Donatella Pastorino, Riz Khan, Jose Barrera, Roxanne Fulcher, Chavah Golden, Deborah Schwartz, Jun Hatsushiba, Gerardo Noriega, Andreas Faserl, Chris Hughes, Laura Upcott, Dan Thomas, Dwight Sowers, Helmut Schroeder, Kathryn Nehlsen, Martijn Meisner, Mladen Dakic, Stephan Somogyi, Rachel England, David Ferron, Chris Berry, Denise Noel, Wil Pannell, Tom McDonough, Steven Boderck, Thomas Garman, Niels Wijdogen, Turki Fahad, Stephan Augustin, Danya Smith, Andy de Vale, Troy Peterson, Ron Mitchell, Steve Clark, Nathan Dye, Melissa McLain, Jean-Baptiste Moretti, Massimo lo Campo, Matteo Bocedi, Kim Gregers Petersen, Randi Rossman, John Hanigosky, Alan Klug, Pietro Moschetta, Jerry Nulton, Daryl Seaton, Michael Kazantsev, Chris Bailey, Kenn Sugiyama, Kevin Long, Kelli Babich, Kevin Goodwin, Chris Cox, Susannah Jaggers, Donald Krstticevic, Monique Beedles, Bryant LaFreniere, Andrei Khitryi, Louise Alexander, Bill Branson, Gustavo Couto, David Alexander, Grant Rykken, Roberto Valenzuela, Claudio Stivala, Brian Wakley, Melanie Woods, Tom McDevitt, Frank Edwards, Donald Geiger, John Sullivan, Joshua Rapoza, Sven Maier, David Bowman, Alwin Dooijeweerd, Samuel Ashby, Ed Swartz, Julio Giron, Jomy Pidiath, Lena Boberg, Birthe Brosolat, Rajkumar Sukhwani, Andrew Noble, Carlos Diaz, Anders Falkeholm, Jose Torres, Nuno Levy, Erik Slinning, Gabor Molnar, Gregory Frank, Gary Manning, Denis Shindin, Jo Ann Gray-Murray, Uwe Loose, Pranjal Dutta, Chris Wozniak, Michael Phillips, Elizabeth Barwell, Brian Johnson, Javier Garcia, James Muir, Lachlan Jackson, Ruslan Spivak, A.B.

Al Mahmood, Christopher Rygh, Colin Dovey, Kweli Sessions, Evan Cohen, Marko Hamel, Scott Ricci, Tessa Silver, Stuart Morse, Gerson Klein, Michael Gottlieb, Don Davis, Hani Al Menaii, Jocelyn Ring, Staci Clarke, Maria Gorelaya, Richard Geller, Morris Pearl, Sebastian Scholz, Karen Forkish, Jama Ball, Nicholas Polachek, Alan Martello, Muhammad Azmil Usol Ghafli, Keith Perrigon, Thomas Vikstrom, Anna Goh, Todd Stuve, Robson Gimenes, Jeremy Freeman, Caroline Chong, Gordon Hardiman, Tom Mackey, Chip Finck, Kishore Krishna, Mike Sigers, Jaime Pena, Stefan Moch, Baba Prasad, Nilesh Patel, Hosung Son, Debra Pickfield, Erle Marion, Jianxiong Zhou, Caryn Ginsberg, Owen Traynor, Deborah Mends, Karin Delin, Paul Gouthro, Nicholas Carrier, Sonya Post, Suhit Anantula, Borut Logar, Blanka Horackova, Tony Downs, Linda Martin, Adrian Leonardi, Sarawut Krataikwan, Mary Lynn Halland, Erik van Triest, Florian Meyer, Luis Martinez, Richard McMurray, Natalia Razumova, Carlisle Connally, Christine Young, Todd Smith, Silas Gimba, Carlos Sanchez-Sicilia, Yutaka Okano, John Mooney, Randy Sugawara, Brad Cleavenger, Lisa Hosokawa, Lesa Nichols, Charles Png, Matthew Hass, Leigh Johnson, Mark Alan Fish, Dave Wood, Mike Williams, Sam Raheel, Lionel Cave, Patrick Hart, Chandrashekar Natarajan, Martine Vanremoortele, Heiner Poelitz, Francisca Salomon, Jeff Chen, Phillip Greene, Colin Collard, Sanjay Shetty, Daniel Lopez, Aaron Coles, Steve Tucker, James Bond, Mark Kirk, Sean Bailey, William Reed, John Schultz, Alexia Moore, Barbara Genius, Eugen Rodel, Pavinee Chuatirarak, Joseph Wiertel, Rebecca Hope, Ken Nakamura, Rick Baca, Gagan Kaul, Laurent Karila, Valeria Castanno, Marco Ossani, John Nunes, Kelly Monroe, Maria Mahar, and Fred Bellier.

A heartfelt thanks to my inspiring team at the NapkinAcademy .com: Xavier Fan, Ai Yat Goh, Deborah DeLue, and Mark Rubin; our weekly calls kept me honest—and on schedule.

Thanks so much to my best business friends: Scott and Becca Williams, Lisa Solomon, Lynn Carruthers, Laila Tarraf, and Andy Grogan.

And I save my greatest thanks for my family, who once again stayed with me all the way: Isabelle, Sophie, and Celeste. I love you. Thank you all.

INDEX